Praise

“Wow! Finally, a sane and [illegible] have been so devastated by gender ideology, and we have had nearly no voice. Lisa Shultz writes about the anguish of parents and especially mothers of daughters. Please read and share this testimony with parents and others who have been impacted by those who subscribe to the ideas of gender and never allow debate or evidence to even be discussed.”

— Jennifer Wesson, Author of *The Gender Party*

“This book is a helpful guide for parents whose children have been captured by radical gender ideology. Shultz identifies the modern trans movement for what it is—a regressive, anti-gay, and anti-woman crusade that reinforces harmful sex stereotypes and irrevocably harms vulnerable people. She joins the voices of the many parents, women, gays, lesbians, and yes, transsexuals who are begging for the broader public to see ‘gender affirming care’ for the medical scandal that it is.”

— Ben Appel, Writer and Journalist

“There is no loss greater than the loss of a child, and in many ways, grieving a living child can be even more tragic. *The Trans Train* is a painful account of losing a child to gender ideology from the perspective of a parent, and it offers real insights into the shattering effects it has on families. But above all, it’s a testament to a mother’s unconditional love for her child, and Lisa offers a compassionate and informative account that will resonate with other parents isolated by this grief.”

— January Littlejohn, Ed.S., LMHC, Parent of Desisted Child

“*The Trans Train* by Lisa Shultz presents a personal narrative combined with a well-referenced examination of the influence of gender ideology in American youth culture and is structured in a way that allows for a chronological understanding of her evolving perspectives. Shultz's storytelling is reflective, providing readers with insights into the challenges she faced in navigating these issues within her family. This book will be particularly helpful for parents who are encountering gender-related language and ideology that is new to them."

—The Genspect Team

"Lisa Shultz has written a passionate account of her family's experience of devastation following her daughter's declaration of a trans identity. It is a story of a loving parent struggling to make sense of the world that seems surreal. A world where a loving parent is the enemy. She shows how this war on reality has real victims."

— Jamie Reed, MS, Clinical Research
Whistleblower from a United States Pediatric Gender Center

"In *The Trans Train*, Lisa Shultz conveys the heartbreak of losing her young adult daughter to a transgender ideology. Her pain is palpable as she tries to understand how her once-thriving child got captured by such a destructive ideology and felt the need to escape her natural body. Any parent who has a gender-questioning child cannot help but deeply relate to her pain and the desire to insulate any young person from this regressive and harmful push to medicalize. Lisa vulnerably shares her own story in enough detail so the reader gets a good sense of the confusion, grief, isolation, anger, and hope for the future in this experience. She also offers many resources to help readers respond to their own family challenges or to help them compassionately support other suffering parents of young people. Parents are often vilified for not doing enough to prevent the harm to their children or for causing the harm in the first place, but through her prose, Lisa demonstrates that parents walk the uncharted journey alone with weights tied to their ankles."

— Kristina Palumbo, Esq., and Erin Friday, Esq., Our Duty–USA

The Trans Train

A Parent's Perspective on
Transgender Medicalization and Ideology

LISA SHULTZ

The Trans Train: A Parent's Perspective on Transgender Medicalization and Ideology

ISBN: 978-0-9986509-8-2
SOCIAL SCIENCE / Gender Studies

I dedicate this book to parents, families, and others who have been harmed, minimized, or canceled when they asked questions or expressed concerns about transgender medicalization and ideology.

Contents

Foreword

IN 1999, I FOUND MYSELF in San Francisco, having finished law school and completing a clerkship with an appellate judge on the East Coast. I fled more than 2,500 miles from home because my friends were all getting married and the relationship I thought would be "the one" had left me with a broken heart. So, I packed my bags and moved to the Bay Area, hoping to start anew and find my perfect match. By the time that happened, I was in my thirties and fantasizing daily about having a child.

When I found out I was pregnant, I could not stop smiling. Everything changed from the moment those two lines appeared on the stick. I stopped dying my hair, eating an unhealthy diet, drinking alcohol, and skiing. I also sold my Jeep Wrangler because of safety concerns ... My body was now my child's. Everything I did was related to ensuring that the fetus grew safely and healthily.

Because of my age, I underwent a CVS test—chorionic villus sample—to test for genetic abnormalities. That test, performed at about six weeks into the pregnancy, not only provides information about chromosomal anomalies but also *confirms* the sex of the baby. Confirms—not "provides an educated guess about" or "assigns"—but provides a scientific fact. Full stop. At least it did in 2003.

Despite living in progressive San Francisco, there were no conversations about whether the baby would be raised without a gender. I was having a boy, pure and simple—XY chromosomes. My leftie mom group and I discussed doulas, water and home births, natural births, birthing plans, and whether playing Mozart really would make our in utero babies smarter. No one talked about our growing babies as having genders other than what their chromosomes revealed: girls or boys. My second pregnancy in 2005 was the same. The CVS test revealed that a baby girl was gestating in my womb. This was an incontrovertible fact. I was to be a mother of a boy and a girl.

In the span of fewer than ten years, every institution, including the legacy media, now describes sex as something that is "assigned": the doctors make a guess, and they could be wrong based upon the future belief of the child. One need not have a medical degree or be a biologist to know that this is a lie.

Every mother fortunate enough to share the experience remembers when her newborn was first placed on her naked chest seconds after being born. Our love affair with our baby continues, and everything we do from that moment forward revolves around nurturing and raising our child. We query friends about pediatricians; we read *Consumer Reports* before we purchase the crib, car seat, stroller, swing, etc.; and we research the best diaper cream and the least toxic sunblock. We leave nothing to chance. Our lives are secondary to that of our children, and it will always be that way until our passing. This is the mother's blessing and curse. A curse because even when the pain is too hard and we want to walk away, we cannot.

Like Lisa's daughter, mine, too, fell sway to gender ideology. Like Lisa, I crumbled and sank into the deepest of despair because I knew that my beautiful daughter was not born wrong. Lisa and I both knew from the moment our daughters took their first sweet breaths that they were perfect. Both of us watched our perfect daughters grow to become perfect young women. Neither of us would accept anything else. We would not collude in our daughters' self-loathing or support their self-harm.*

As you read *The Trans Train*, you will get a window into the unfathomable pain a mother experiences when her child believes her body is wrong, when she believes that happiness will only be attained by mimicking the other sex and indulging in fantastical medical interventions that will neither change her sex nor resolve her self-hatred. A mother of a trans-identified adult child can only sit back and watch her child die by a thousand cuts while the world cheers on her destruction. There is no solace for the parent. The parent suffers alone.

The gender cult will fall, leaving oceans of grief and regret. When the truth finally spills out, those who created the gender juggernaut will most likely walk away without much, if any, retribution. There will be no apologies to the young adults who have irreversibly harmed their bodies—"You consented, you asked for it, and we just gave you want you wanted" will be their defense.

The major medical associations will hold the World Professional Association of Transgender Health responsible—"You're the experts. We're just lobbyists looking out for our members. We're not responsible for patients' well-being. It's up to the doctors and patients to decide the best course for the patient."

**My daughter avoided any medicalization because her transgender identity appeared when she was a young teenager, allowing me the time and control to redirect her worst impulses. At age 15, she returned to comfort in her female body.*

The politicians will point at the medical community—"You told us that transitioning was lifesaving, that it was reversible, and that gender-confused people would commit suicide. We just made the laws you told us were needed."

The schools will point at the politicians—"You forced us to affirm a student's identity, to deceive parents about their child's struggles with gender dysphoria, and to see parents as almost certain abusers. We were just following orders."

The mental health providers will also blame the politicians—"You warned us that we had to affirm or we would be in violation of anti-conversion therapy laws—laws that were twisted to ensure that gay children uneasy with their budding sexuality would have their homosexuality 'transitioned' out of them, depriving them of their basic human rights."

The corporations will claim they were just exploiting capitalistic needs to increase profits by using transgenderism in their advertising. The corporations will blame the nonprofits who score them on their dedication to environmental, social, and governance practices, and the most cost-effective method of attaining high scores was to throw a few Pride parades.

Universities will claim they were trying to be inclusive, combat discrimination, and promote civil rights and bodily autonomy.

The pharmaceutical companies will claim ignorance—"We didn't know that doctors were prescribing our drugs for off-label usage, and we certainly did not advertise them as we silently watched our coffers overflow. Plus, the Dutch told us (our manufactured) hormones were safe and effective."

Significant investors will respond that it's not their job to invest in humanist pursuits—profits first—gender is a billion-dollar industry.

The legacy media will respond that they are just reporters, just reporting the facts—even if those facts were only from one side of the argument.

Yes, when it all falls, they will all bicker over which group was to blame for the transitioning of the most vulnerable children and adults in a generation already damaged by the oppressor narrative, online porn, and social media algorithms herding them toward dissociation and rejection of self ... Then they will collectively turn their eyes toward the parents—the mothers, in particular—sneering and pointing. It was the mother's fault, they will say.

Mothers will be blamed, regardless of whether they capitulated to their child's transgender identity or pushed back against it. They either fell for the ideology's doctrines or did not fight hard enough to save their children. Lisa's story exemplifies the impossible task of parenting a child who is determined to ruin her perfectly healthy body while the transgender world is cheering on her destruction.

I encourage you to read and share this parent's contribution to the growing concern and outrage about the harms of medicalization being pushed on our kids. It is time to stop the trans train. Lisa offers an awareness of this devastating trend and its far-reaching effects on our children and their families, and she provides resources to guide you to learn more.

— Erin Friday, Esq.
Our Duty–USA
December 2023

Why I Wrote This Book

MY EXPERIENCE AS A PARENT whose young adult daughter needed time, exploration of treatment options, and healing of multiple issues but instead clambered aboard the medicalized trans train has led me to feel like I'm in a tortured dream state. Parental struggle such as mine is hidden from most people. We live in virtual isolation except for private support groups and a few dear friends. Any version of losing a child is every parent's worst nightmare. This nightmare has a name, and it is transgender ideology and their partnership with the gender affirmation care system, which encourages medicalization for kids who self-identify as trans.

It still shocks me when I realize how fast and furious this movement overtakes young people and families. One moment, you are enjoying time together, and the next moment, those relationships are broken. When trans ideology comes to a family, it is like a bomb drops and relationships are decimated, the profound ripple effects spreading from the point of detonation. The "care" is missing from the model, replaced by profits and urgings from strangers to move forward with medicalized procedures and medications that are difficult, even impossible, to reverse if the person changes her mind, underlying issues resurface, or she suffers too much from social ramifications or the adverse effects of testosterone and surgery.

Even when raised by a loving parent, a young adult may be influenced to the point of hopping on the fast-moving trans train and leaving the loving family behind. If the trans ideology can touch my family, it can touch anyone's. Sharing my views is a risk I'm willing to take if it can be used to help others.

The biggest decision of a young person's life, to present themselves as the opposite sex, needs time and a thorough investigation of the root causes prompting the request for the drastic measures of drugs and permanent surgery to remove healthy body parts. As this book was being written in 2023, the voice of "affirming parents" has been amplified by the media, particularly liberal-leaning outlets. Dissenting parent voices such as mine, bringing up valid questions, are usually ignored or canceled. I wish to discuss a full range of harm that seems to be occurring across multiple sectors of society by transgender ideology, as well as the collective parental trauma of losing a child in this manner.

This book reflects my beliefs, yet my friends comprise a vast array of ideologies. I have friends with liberal and conservative viewpoints and every perspective in between. I have friends who are atheists and friends who practice Christianity, Judaism, and a full range of religious beliefs. I consider myself spiritual yet open minded. Politically, my perspective comes from the middle. I became disillusioned with both political parties many years ago, and now I am registered to vote as an Independent. I am put off by the righteousness often expressed by each party and sad that there seems to be a war between political parties in the US. The polarization of our country troubles me greatly.

I was devastated and in deep grief after helplessly watching while I lost my daughter in 2022–2023. Many years ago when I divorced, friends and family gave me support, hugs, meals, flowers, and thoughtful cards. But when I finally told people I had lost my youngest daughter in this way, I was essentially on my own without much support. People didn't know what to say (and I can't blame them), so most gave me advice to see a therapist, go to church, or just accept what my daughter chose to do. Some people dismissed my reasons for grief and distanced themselves from me. A few family members championed my daughter's transition. Those who supported the drastic measures taking place, including the mastectomy, did so either without talking with me or while fully knowing my concerns but championing her rapid medicalization path anyway.

When I woke each morning, I said to myself, "Oh my God, this nightmare is real." As a way of processing my complex feelings as a parent, I began journaling in 2022, and this writing became a consistent practice in 2023. I thought about what I wanted to say day and night. I captured my thoughts on paper. Then I tried to put those entries into a meaningful order and presentation. I conducted exhaustive research as I wrote. Much of what I had been doing prior to 2023 lost most of its importance. My whole paradigm of purpose had shifted, and I looked at everything around me differently.

When I look at the US now, I am devastated and angry that we live in a country that supports the narrative that it is okay to medicalize young girls and women by prescribing testosterone and performing mastectomies as a first response to the girls' gender confusion, stress, or mental health concerns. I am flabbergasted that loving moms who ask questions and express concerns about this strategy have been labeled as hateful and transphobic. I am distressed that society seemingly devalues moms and family members who lovingly question the affirmation care model and its treatment of our teens and young women.

A note about terminology for breast removal: I use the word "mastectomy" throughout this book instead of "top surgery." For a girl or young woman who believes she is trapped in the wrong body and that "female" was an arbitrary assignment at birth, she might prefer to think of a mastectomy as a masculizing surgery. Using the term "top surgery" probably feels better than "mastectomy" for those young women, as well as for gender affirmation care clinics and the surgeon. However, no one is born in the wrong body. A girl may elect to have her breasts removed due to a lack of acceptance of her body, but deciding to cut off this healthy body part does not change her innate biological reality. Mastectomies aren't lifesaving for a newly trans-identifying girl, and kids often regret the loss of their breasts, some suing the surgeons and medical providers who removed them.[1] Surgery enables body loathing and dishonors one's natural body. This mastectomy craze of removing healthy breasts that is happening to our young girls and women today will probably be the era that we look back on in the future and ask ourselves how and why we ever allowed and glorified self-harm.

I Hope to Help Others

It pains me to provide personal details in this book. My life and that of my family is private. I have tried to keep personal examples to a minimum. I've learned that my story is so common that I can speak broadly of the effects of transgender ideology, as parent stories are incredibly similar worldwide.*

**Throughout this book, I interchange "I" and "we" because I represent myself and many other parents.*

It is my hope that this book might support other parents and families in their times of turmoil around the gender transition of their daughter or son. I aim to show the bigger picture. I encourage gender care providers and those stuck in the "affirmation-only" model to look down the road and envision a future where a transitioned person may be experiencing complications of testosterone and mastectomies and hysterectomies for the rest of their lives. Imagine their lives as older adults with broken family relationships. Speculate on how their untreated trauma or mental issues will surface despite their placement on the shelf of not needing investigation and further attention. What will happen when those issues get triggered or come out later due to stress, loss, and time, especially if they have cut off ties with non-affirming family members? How will that person be able to effectively handle life's challenges? How will the gender affirming care community fix the mess they have created? Will those who participated in medical/surgical interventions, as well as healthcare practitioners and insurance companies involved, be there to pick up the pieces if regret surfaces?

Many families have been emotionally blackmailed and told that they will lose their kids to suicide if they don't agree to participate in the affirmation model. This threat is an unsubstantiated claim. When parents tap into the experiences of detransitioners, they learn that mental health often crumbles after transition. If it doesn't work out so well on the other side, then what? It is a no-win situation for parents.

I am aware and can respect that there are many variations of gender presentations, dress, and interests. No one needs to adhere to rigid stereotypes. I also realize that within a same-sex relationship, each partner may express themselves in a more masculine or feminine way. Heterosexual people can also present themselves in more traditional feminine or masculine ways, such as by the careers and activities they choose and by their clothing and hairstyles. I am in favor of all those personal choices, but I am against the rush to medicalize our children and young people to present as the opposite sex when they are confused or when other conditions, such as autism, are misattributed as "trans." I am disturbed by transgender activism, which undermines women and places demands on families, institutions, and society. Transgender ideology seems to be an agenda to disrupt and destabilize society and threaten and dismantle organizations and the family, and so this movement does not have my support.

On an individual basis, unless one has worked to address their feelings and issues through years of therapy and other gentle, natural options, and unless one has examined the personality, past, and underlying issues, as well as the relationship with social media, then healthy body parts should not be cut off. We are harming our children and pretending we are helping them when we do not allow them time to mature. They also need time to reflect and consider the lifelong consequences of their decisions. Solid critical thinking skills need to be developed and honed over time. In-person interactions need to be prioritized over screen time. Again, I hope this book helps people to pause the process and thoughtfully consider all options and the bigger picture of the effects of transgender ideology.

Who This Book Is For

I hope the insights and research in this book will be valuable for parents who are encountering difficult-to-understand gender-related language and ideology that doesn't make sense to them. Parents who are grasping to understand the sweeping changes they witness in their child, in the schools, and in society. Parents who may be shaken and need fortification and reassurance that it is a natural response to express concern despite being told it is not acceptable to question. Parents who share the agony and devastation of losing a child to this destructive ideology, as I have. The book may also appeal to others who wish to learn more and support hurting parents and kids harmed by the trans train.

What I Hope the Future Holds

I hope to see those who participate in the gender affirming care model switch to engaging in the examination of deeper issues and the exploration of other treatment options beyond immediate transition when gender confusion presents itself. Young people may need support with counseling to understand and heal from the root cause of their feelings and experiences of dysphoria. James Esses, writer, commentator, and co-founder of Thoughtful Therapists, shares, "We have taken a mental health condition, affecting a relatively small proportion of the population, and extrapolated it out to the entirety of society. Rather than being taught that gender dysphoria is a mental health condition, children are being taught that every person alive has a unique gender identity."[2]

I hope that practitioners will stop muddying the waters by prescribing testosterone and scheduling a mastectomy as the first and sometimes only treatment choice, which negates possible complex and nuanced past traumas, comorbidities, or mental issues. Could gender distress be exacerbated with an extreme focus on it instead of a broad look at life and other perspectives? I hope such practitioners become aware that an affirmation-only policy might be enabling maladaptive behaviors and worsening underlying conditions by ignoring them.

I also hope that the gender affirming practitioners and the greed of those who profit from this medicalized pathway that's destroying families and harming our young people will be exposed. I hope they will be held accountable for this medical scandal. Time will tell. I hope I live to see it.

This book also explores what is happening to women's rights due to the controversy of gender ideology. I was interested in how biology got usurped in favor of gender self-identification and how the trans agenda affects parts of society such as lesbian, gay, bi, and transsexual groups. This book hopes to be thought-provoking and a launchpad to open your eyes to the wide array of mindsets and beliefs. The trans ideology trend and narrative happening throughout the world will soon reach you if it hasn't already, so I hope that learning more about it now will be valuable in how you might respond to it when it affects you in some way.

The resource section at the back of the book is another avenue for exploration, and each site includes more resources (and rabbit holes) to explore.

Although my personal perspective cannot possibly represent all parents' views, I hope that other discarded and devastated parents will feel less alone as they read this book. It's not only my story; it represents the story of thousands of people. Marian Wright Edelman said it well: "Be a good ancestor. Stand for something bigger than yourself."

Thank you for taking the time to read this parental perspective, which is the tip of the iceberg on the bigger tragedy unfolding within families and other groups throughout the world. When a drastic and rushed medicalization approach based on trending controversial ideology is presented as the only option to solve the emotional, psychological, or physical discomfort of our kids, then we have failed to help the younger generation set themselves up for future health and well-being.

Introduction

A PARENT CAN LOSE A CHILD in many ways: accident, suicide, gun violence, child trafficking, kidnapping, alcoholism, drug addiction, or the opioid epidemic, to name a few. These are all black holes of devastation and tragedy. I would never have imagined that a new way would spring up and threaten to take our kids and that it would happen so quickly and at an alarmingly increasing rate. I especially would never have imagined that it would take my child and devastate my family.

This new black hole is disguised as an enlightened movement of progressive thinkers and advocates for social justice that are capturing kids through social media and early exposure to gender identity ideology at school. Many of our educational systems, medical organizations, and governments worldwide are participating in and supporting the movement. It's called gender ideology,[3] which denies the reality of sex as binary and instead fosters the belief that children can be born in the wrong body and may identify with a different "gender." This ideology, which places demands on society, organizations, and individuals, is highly controversial and is rapidly becoming a scandal because it is causing upheaval in families, schools, sports, medicine, law, and religious and political groups. Once your child, adolescent, or young adult gets sucked into this vortex, they are at risk of boarding a fast-moving train called the trans train.

As a mom, I feel compelled to ask questions. Why are girls demanding the drug testosterone in skyrocketing numbers? Why are so many young girls and women getting mastectomies? What is happening when the young woman's scarred mastectomy chest is glorified? Why is there a new industry profiting from removing any traces of femininity from our daughters? Why are women losing their safe spaces and rights? Why is this drastic medicalized trend rushed, creating a destructive trans train that roars fast and furious, ignoring the whole person, their history, and their family?

Before we explore this topic further, please know that I am a loving mother, an open-minded woman, and a person who believes that everyone has the right to live life as they wish. Everyone whose family has been touched by gender ideology has a unique experience and perspective, which I respect. My purpose in sharing my experience and perspective is to provide information that may help another individual and family to slow down the train and make decisions carefully. There's no need to rush life-changing, body-altering decisions that are difficult or impossible to reverse. If even one person chooses to slow it down or grind the medicalized trans train to a halt to consider the ramifications, then my risk of sharing my story and putting my perspective out there will have been worth it.

I also wish to acknowledge that there are good people participating in this harmful ideology through their workplaces, and they may have been deceived or forced to comply with gender identity rhetoric or lose their jobs. Maybe some who affirmed did not understand the full ramifications of their alignment with an inadequate care model regarding the long-term health and well-being of the child. Perhaps some participants had good intentions of inclusion and diversity. But whatever it once was, now is the time to stop participating. Parents are beyond frustrated and disappointed in the affirmation-only stance and the individuals and institutions that subscribe to it because it has harmed our kids and our families, as well as society. Only allowing affirmation indicates that a child's feelings are facts, and we believe that feelings, which are often transient, are not facts. One may hold respect and empathy for those suffering from gender confusion and still say no to a destructive ideology that advocates the medicalization of kids. Everyone involved in our children's transition failed to adequately address or treat the full range of each child's complex personality and history. The affirmation care model and those involved in it also failed to preserve the precious parent-child bond.

When I was at the beginning of this journey, I had to quickly learn the lingo of the gender identity language. Perhaps you are at the beginning, too. Below are definitions of key terms that may help you understand this new and ever-changing ideology. Please note: Because the language changes so rapidly, it is possible that my references to definitions will not be the same in future years as they were at the time of this book's publication. The language of this ideology is also highly controversial, so inevitably, critical readers may differ in their opinions of the words used within this book. Through my research, here is my understanding of the nuances of the word "trans" to shed light on the distinction of terms that are often lumped together in use and understanding.

Transvestite

Transvestite is when someone occasionally or frequently cross-dresses to appear as the opposite sex.

Transsexual

Transsexual refers to someone who is distressed with their biology and wishes to align with the opposite sex with hormonal and surgical procedures to alleviate suffering and to function in the world. These individuals have undergone medical interventions.

Transgender or "Trans"

Transgender, "trans" for short, is an adjective denoting or relating to a person who believes their gender identity does not correspond to their natal sex, their anatomical sex organs, or their DNA. It usually refers to someone who does not believe in innate biology and believes babies are arbitrarily assigned a sex at birth. As a result, one can self-identify with any gender they wish at any time. These individuals may or may not have undergone medical interventions. They are usually, but not always, children or young adults. This is the category in which this book places its focus.

The Trans Train

This term was first used in a multi-part documentary entitled *Sweden's U-Turn on Trans Kids: The Trans Train: The New Patient Group & Regretters*. The YouTube video description reads: "In May of 2021, Sweden announced a change of their policy regarding the medical and surgical transition of children. The change came in the wake of several bombshell documentaries which explored the issue of medicalization of children experiencing gender dysphoria in Sweden and Europe."[4]

For the purposes of this book, I am describing a trans train as a medicalized pathway to altering one's body to look more like the opposite sex. This is the fast-moving train that took away my daughter. It typically begins with using cross-sex hormones to modify one's external appearance. The next step is surgery, which removes healthy body parts such as breasts, female reproductive organs, and male genitalia in adolescents and young adults.

In my case, my daughter went from beginning to take testosterone to a surgical mastectomy—all in less than one year. Research shows that in many cases, such as mine, underlying conditions were minimized or not addressed by physicians prescribing testosterone or recommending and performing surgery. Little or no effort is made to uncover or treat childhood trauma, relationship loss, an eating disorder, gender confusion, or underlying mental conditions. Those multiple, complex issues often take many experts, approaches, and years of treatment and healing to reach a healthy place. But instead of taking the time to care for each issue, the gender industry's first line of treatment for young women is to immediately prescribe the body-altering drug testosterone.

Loving, concerned parents and family members are cast out of the discussions during this fast ride if they advocate exploring other options and therapy. Transgender advocates and allies label parents as uneducated, unsafe, toxic, and transphobic if they do not affirm their child's self-identification with the opposite gender of their biological, natal sex. This was my experience, too, and I didn't participate, affirm, or celebrate this transformation because it was occurring way too fast and without exploring more beneficial and less-invasive alternatives for my daughter. I have now experienced cancel culture firsthand. I was told that I may not express concerns or ask questions about the trans progression of my daughter. The trans advocate community seems to find few parents of value unless they affirm without question. Those who express concern or resistance to a child or family member's decision to engage in chemical or surgical interventions are effectively "canceled."

Several years before my daughter boarded the trans train, I started to hear from a few friends who were experiencing their family's unraveling as their kids became unrecognizable. As I listened to their stories, I thought to myself, "Dear God, may this ideology not come to my family." And then it did.

When I found out that my daughter had gotten on the trans train, I joined support groups, and I was shocked to discover that thousands of parents had also lost their kids to the trans movement. Sadly, I was not alone, and the stories within the group were eerily similar. Although I wrote this book from my personal perspective as a mom, please know that thousands of other parents worldwide are going through a similar heart-wrenching experience. Another parent within a support group I participate in expressed the following, and I can relate:

> *"I lay awake at 3 a.m., or I've never even made it to peaceful sleep, thinking about what the world is prepared to do to him, to his perfect, healthy, beautiful body. Unimaginable horrors that I can't shut off. The torture of a beloved child. The torture of a loving parent. This world has gone bad. Become unbelievably cruel." — Elliott Swimmer*

This trend is not a conservative versus liberal or Christian versus secular issue. Kids throughout the world with different political, religious, and cultural beliefs all have access to the same online ideology, can be affected by social contagion, and are often coached by social media influencers. These vulnerable kids and young adults might have a different underlying condition, but the result is the same: they are pulled onto the trans train by friends and social media influencers and also pushed onto the trans train by people who consider themselves social justice warriors or are connected with the pharmaceutical and medical industry desiring profit from this demographic. Often, there is virtually no acknowledgment or treatment of the underlying conditions, and frequently, there is encouragement to sever ties with caring and loving parents and family members who express doubt about the long-term well-being this pathway is promising.

It usually begins with a kid's self-diagnosis and proclamation of trans because they feel they were born in the wrong body after watching videos on YouTube, TikTok, and other platforms and interacting with social media influencers promoting gender identity ideology. They may secretly socially transition at school before they tell their parents. Fast forward, and the family finds a situation in which a whole medical system, in the name of gender affirmation care (GAC), rallies around the kid and alienates the parents.

No one is born in the wrong body; it seems some are just born in the wrong era when the natural body is no longer respected. Kids today are born into an era where gender identity ideology threatens to take away their right to mature naturally through puberty and into adulthood without damaging and altering their healthy bodies. The sanctity of the male and female body is in jeopardy.

There is a significant lack of evidence that cross-sex hormones and surgical procedures, such as mastectomies, that attempt to chemically and cosmetically alter biological sex are effective solutions to young women's difficulties. Transgender medicalization is an experiment that might have dire consequences for the future of our children and society. Furthermore, trans medicalization is not lifesaving in most cases. I have great empathy for parents who were told, without evidence, that their kids would commit suicide if they didn't affirm their new cross-sex identification. Ideology that pushes the concept that sex is arbitrarily assigned at birth and that innate biology can be switched is harmful to our kids, their health, and their futures.

Someone may choose to present themselves in appearance as the opposite sex, but their chromosomes will always represent their biological sex, which was determined prior to birth and confirmed at birth. If one is confused about biological reality and has been told it can be altered, they have been misinformed and misled.

The biological reality is that human sex is binary and immutable as female and male, even if an individual presents themself otherwise. Nonbinary, where one chooses not to present as either sex or to present as the opposite sex, is a personal choice, but it does not change chromosomal structure. It is not possible to change one's sex. We may empathize with those who have disassociated with their biological reality and seek to understand the cause of this thought process, but it crosses the line when history is rewritten and self-harm is encouraged and applauded. Most people understand these principles but have lost their freedom of speech due to threats by trans activists to be silent or lose their jobs, positions, businesses, professional licenses, organizations, and other valued livelihoods.

Social transition is not harmless; it places the child on the boarding platform of the trans train. Affirming the child's self-declaration of feeling like the opposite sex may buy them a ticket for the train ride to their self-destruction. Trans is not the "new gay" because gay is same-sex attraction, which does not involve the removal of healthy body parts. Medicalization creates permanent drug dependency and a plethora of health problems for life. The GAC model minimizes risks, and the trans ideology promises happiness with a new body that is unrecognizable as their former selves. It sounds ludicrous, but it is happening every day.

If you haven't lost a child or young adult yet, count yourself lucky. If your kid is dabbling in this trend, act fast to understand everything you can about it. There's a big difference between experimenting with cross-dressing and expressions of looking like the opposite of one's natal sex, and the medical model that hooks young people into a lifelong dependency on hormone injections, prescription pills, or creams and then surgically alters them and sends them out into the world without the slightest care about the lifelong impact of those medical interventions.

Parents, if you are new to this movement, you don't have time to leisurely wait and see what happens. At least turn your questions and concerns into quickly educating and empowering yourself, as you may provide your child's only encouragement to critically think through their decision. Once the train takes off from the station of puberty blockers, next up is a cross-sex hormone prescription, meaning your child will be jabbing their leg with a syringe full of synthetic hormones, then the mastectomy (breast removal) often happens in less than a year if they are no longer a minor, as was the case with my daughter. The trans train is designed for affirmation only, and if you ask questions or express concerns, you will likely be ostracized or cut out of your child's life. Parents who don't agree may be discarded along with their daughter's healthy breast tissue or their son's genitalia.

This book is my contribution to giving voice to the brokenhearted, anguished, and traumatized parents whose worlds have fallen apart. This book begs the reader to stop blanketly enabling and participating in ideology that promotes medicalized interventions. The sacred bond of parent and child is being compromised. Families are unraveling. Girls and women, both straight and lesbian, are particularly affected by gender ideology; they are losing their rights, safe spaces, and fairness in sports. Mastectomies for healthy girls and young women, and the glorification of those scars, is a blight in human history and must stop.

Before we go on, I will present a few more terms for readers who are new to the lingo connected with trans.

Gender Dysphoria

Gender dysphoria describes a sense of unease or confusion that a person may have because they perceive a mismatch between their biological sex and their gender identity. Dysphoria is complex and difficult to explain to someone not experiencing it.

Not all individuals experiencing dysphoria go to the extreme of a full medical and surgical intervention to appear like the opposite sex. Some people prefer a genderless look. A gender-neutral person usually prefers the pronouns they/their/them. This neutral position might also be referred to as nonbinary, meaning they do not wish to conform to stereotypical male or female presentations.

You may also have heard the term "fluid" within gender ideology. Those who identify as gender fluid say they can be male one day, female another day, both male and female, or neither.

Social Transition and Medical Transition

For those new to all the gender lingo, there are stages to transitioning. According to the website of UC San Francisco Trans Care, social transition comprises the following:

Social Transition

- Presenting in public part time or full time in one's non-natal gender may include:
  - Changing your wardrobe or hairstyle

    - Packing (using a penile prosthesis to give a masculine genital contour)
    - Tucking (placing the testes into the inguinal canal, held in place with tight underwear or a garment called a gaff, to give a feminine genital contour)
    - Binding (using a tight chest garment to flatten breasts and give a masculine chest contour)
    - Breast, hip, or buttock prostheses (inserts into clothing or bra to augment breast, hip, or buttock size)
- Coming out to spouse, partner(s), children, friends, family, classmates, coworkers, or community members
- Changing your legal documents to reflect your chosen name, gender identity, and pronoun used[5]

After a social transition, some girls and women move into medical transition, which may consist of part or all of the following: removal of breast tissue (mastectomy), removal of the ovaries and uterus (oophorectomy and hysterectomy), and the construction of a penis and scrotum (metoidioplasty, phalloplasty, and scrotoplasty).

Medicalization Transition

Helpful Professor published an article on June 26, 2023, entitled *12 Medicalization Examples*, written by Paul C. Gregory and peer-reviewed by Chris Drew. The author defines medicalization as "the act of excessively defining and medically treating conditions, behaviors, or attitudes."

Gregory continues, "This phenomenon has occurred when medical professionals, pharmaceutical drug manufacturers, and other relevant expert panels attempt to apply medical rationalization to situations where medical intervention may not be in the best interest of an individual."

The article offers examples of medicalization, including:

1. ***Medicalization of Depression:*** Instead of using non-pharmacological treatments like psychotherapy, lifestyle adjustments, or holistic treatments, depression is medically diagnosed and drugs are prescribed to the patient as a first option.
2. ***Medicalization of ADHD:*** ADHD is immediately diagnosed, then treated with medication; social interventions or education-driven approaches are dismissed.
3. ***Medicalization of Menopause:*** Although it is a normal part of the female aging process, menopause has been medicalized as a disease, which has led to medical professionals encouraging women to take hormone replacement drugs.

Other types of medicalizations mentioned are sleep disorders, bad breath, normal aging, shyness, obesity, restless leg syndrome, acne, and substance abuse.[6] Perhaps you, like me, are not a proponent of medicalization as the first option for most conditions. There may be solid reasons to use a medicalized model if other avenues are thoroughly explored and exhausted, but it's often the first-choice treatment provided by the medical community desiring financial profit from engaging in the model. This model seems to be prevalent in the medicalization of trans-identifying youth, a for-profit medical industry that is capitalizing on distressed youth who desire quick-fix remedies to their complex problems.[7] The medicalized "care" is invasive, as it involves making kids and young adults drug-dependent on testosterone or estrogen and also removes healthy breast tissue and male genitalia, sometimes rendering the young people sterile.

On a personal note, which may be helpful in understanding my perspective, neither my mom nor I had any cosmetic work done on our faces or bodies. We allowed ourselves to age naturally using minimal makeup and without having fillers, Botox, or plastic surgery. We declined the medicalization pathway of anti-aging procedures that are endless and expensive. I carefully consider my options before going down any rabbit hole of medicalization, and I generally prefer to let nature take its course with me.

Detransition

This term describes when someone who once cross-sex identified has changed their mind. It's the cessation or reversal of a transgender identification or gender transition by social, legal, or medical means. For example, a biologically born female transitioned socially and medically by dressing as a man, taking testosterone, and having a mastectomy, and then attempts to return to her natal sex as a woman. This reversal may entail returning to wearing women's clothing, ceasing testosterone injections, and sometimes undergoing breast reconstruction surgery.

Desister

This term describes a person who previously experienced gender confusion and identified as transgender but decides not to transition and instead re-identifies with their natal sex prior to medical intervention.

I feel sad that so many young people seem to be tortured with gender confusion and dysphoria. Puberty and adolescence can be difficult to navigate. Some kids have experienced sexual trauma or abuse. Their pain and body loathing must be severe to want to bind or cut off body parts to try to fix their suffering. They may also have same-sex attraction and find that orientation to be challenging to accept.

Let us question why we are losing so many teenage girls and young women to an ideology that encourages them to discard all things that represent womanhood and motherhood. Moms are often thrown out, along with the young women's healthy breast tissue. Being a woman is a gift if not rejected. Could it be that rebellion and individuation have been taken to the extreme by transgender-presenting youth? Could some kids who identify as transgender be rallying against gender stereotypes and wish to make a countercultural statement? Could this extremism negatively boomerang back on them? Might our educational institutions, therapists, and doctors be failing our teenagers and young women?

I am not aware of any other mental or medical condition in which a kid or young adult self-diagnoses themselves after social media and internet engagement, undergoes no objective testing, and then receives irreversible medication and surgery upon demand. Parents like me have legitimate questions, and we are tired of being shut out of the conversation!

I will ask over and over until I die why doctors, therapists, school educators, and counselors are not looking deeply at the individual in front of them and creating a treatment plan with options that heal trauma, offer tools and adaptive coping strategies to navigate their emotional life, and address underlying mental issues before placing that young person on a rapid medicalization pathway that ignores complex dynamics of their personality and experiences. Why is there a perseveration on gender instead of expanding inquiry and addressing all dimensions of a being in distress? Why are we enabling kids to possibly run from something such as past trauma or encouraging distraction from emotional pain by quickly writing a prescription for puberty blockers or a cross-sex hormone on the first or second visit to a clinic?

The world holds a lot of hurting people. With proper care, support, and therapy, many of those hurting people can overcome the pain and heal from deep trauma, relationship losses, and mental issues. Gay youth and young adults need acceptance of their same-sex attraction. It is unacceptable to engage in the erasure of gay orientation. Something is terribly wrong when natural and holistic measures to relieve emotional struggles are left untouched in favor of lifelong, irreversible medical interventions that are experimental, expensive, and come with a host of additional adverse effects. I believe that those who participate in this harmful direction without differential diagnosis and the examination of commonalities are irresponsible.

What This Book Does Not Include

- *Details about boys and young men who transition.* The only reason is that I don't have boys, so I don't have experience in that area. I also won't be discussing the effects of estrogen on boys. Someone else can write a book about boys; however, I suspect that many of the issues I bring up will be similar to issues experienced by parents of boys wishing to present themselves as girls.
- *Information on the impact of sex change on children before puberty.* While the information is mounting that puberty blockers are not reversible and they harm a child's development, I don't have experience with puberty blockers because my daughter transitioned in her twenties. If you search, you can find many stories about young kids who switched to presenting as the opposite sex before they even had a chance

to mature through puberty and time. Today, if a young child is expressing an interest in identifying as the opposite sex, they are often given puberty blockers initially and then funneled into a progression of cross-sex hormones and surgeries. I wonder if they were provided with support rather than ushered onto a medical path, might they grow up with an intact, healthy body and express themselves as gay? Again, the topic of converting little kids to another sex before they hit puberty is reserved for another author.

- *Examples of school systems undermining parental concerns.* Because my daughter graduated from university before she transitioned, I am not able to address the issues in school systems. However, I am disturbed by hearing multiple stories of educators and school counselors undermining parental concerns. Often, the school's philosophy is to socially transition children without notifying parents and make it sound like the school is a safe place and home is not. If a child declares they wish to identify as the opposite sex, and if a parent doesn't affirm and adopt a child's new name and pronouns, then Child Protective Services (CPS) can be called. CPS may declare that non-affirming parents are guilty of emotional abuse and neglect and may suggest that the child be removed and rehomed to an affirming foster care family. This new family may be called a *glitter family*, defined as:

An ideologically aligned group of people who convince a child that their natal family does not love them because they're not affirming them, but that they will love and affirm the child.[8]

- *My daughter's preferred pronouns.* I have elected to address my daughter as a daughter and to use she/her pronouns instead of masculine or neutral (they/them/their) pronouns throughout this book. I intend no disrespect. This book relays my experience, and I have chosen to speak in a way that honors the natal sex of the child that I, her mother, vividly remember giving birth to. This is my choice to lessen confusion in this book. Also, my generation generally prefers to use singular pronouns for one person instead of plural. And finally, the use of pronouns by a trans-identifying person tends to change based on how they feel and where they are in the process of their transition, so I am sticking with feminine pronouns for consistency and clarity.

The Trans Train is my attempt to show, from my viewpoint, what this devastating, dystopian train trip encompasses for my family and for many others. I am not a journalist or a counselor, and I do not work in the mental health field. I am not an expert in transgender ideology. However, when I want to learn about a topic, I dig in. I read multiple books, listened to podcasts, and watched several films. I researched websites and articles. I joined multiple professional and parent groups. I listened to detransitioners, who provided valuable perspectives on the current transgender movement. I attended a Genspect conference, hearing from multiple doctors, therapists, biologists, and other professionals. I dug into social media platforms and read countless websites and Substacks on the topic of gender. (See the Resource section at the back of the book for further information.)

I am a devoted and loving mother sharing my story to help others. I was not able to cover every aspect connected to this nuanced topic because the number of rabbit holes is vast. I focused on issues from my experience with my daughter, from the experiences of other families in similar situations, and from my research. To the best of my abilities, I have attempted to properly quote and cite others within this book. Thank you for witnessing and listening to my perspective.

A Parent's Confusion

PARENTS OFTEN EXPERIENCE SHOCK when their daughter proclaims, often quite suddenly, that she is really a boy. The girl might say she feels she is trapped in the wrong body. During her announcement, she may insist that she be referred to by a new name and pronouns. If she is a minor, still living at home, and really in a hurry to jump on the trans train, she may ask her mom to buy her a breast compression binder before her mom has even digested the news. If the girl's appearance hasn't evolved already, she may request boys' clothing and a short haircut. Then, the daughter may demand that she start taking a prescription for testosterone immediately.

After the parents' initial shock at such a proclamation, they first move into a state of confusion. They might ask themselves how they missed all the signs that their girl felt like a boy and evaluate all the previous years of their daughter's life in their minds. Parents may also evaluate friend influences because sometimes a cluster of friends declares they are nonbinary or trans around the same time period. It is the beginning of sleepless nights and confusion for the parents, who often turn to the internet to do research and try to understand what is happening to their daughter and their family. Frequently, parents find the term "ROGD," or rapid-onset gender dysphoria, a term coined by Dr. Lisa Littman. It refers to the gender dysphoria that occurs after exposure to transgender-related social media and to people and friends who identify as transgender.

The website by SEGM, Society for Evidence-Based Gender Medicine, includes an article entitled "Study of 1,655 Cases Supports the 'Rapid-Onset Gender Dysphoria' Hypothesis: Parents report a deterioration in children's mental health and intrafamilial bonds following transition." The article says:

> *The ROGD hypothesis suggests that the recent surge in transgender-identifying adolescents is explained, at least in part, by a rise in the number of previously gender-normative teens who developed gender-related distress in response to various psychosocial factors (e.g., mental health conditions, internalized homophobia, trauma, etc.). Opponents of the ROGD hypothesis claim that the surge is merely the result of greater acceptance of transgender identities by society, and hence, a greater willingness among "intrinsically transgender" adolescents to "come out."*[9]

And so it begins. Parents must sift through the highly controversial subject of transgender ideology and make sense of it.

My daughter was a twenty-eight-year-old young woman when she told me she was trans. No matter the kid's age when trans ideology touches the family, the parents and other family members will start to research it. I will share what my internet digging produced in case it helps to speed up the learning curve for newly shell-shocked parents, those who wish to understand more about this issue, or those who are hoping to avoid being blindsided.

Note: I suggest reading the book *Parents with Inconvenient Truths about Trans: Tales from the Home Front in the Fight to Save Our Kids.* This book applies to a large swath of parental experiences, particularly for the younger age group of pre-teens and adolescents.

In my research, I am seeing strange paradoxes in the realm of gender ideology. Currently, if a therapist makes inquiries about the root causes of gender dysphoria, they are called conversion therapists, but if a surgeon removes breasts or male genitalia of a teen or young adult in an attempt to change the outward appearance of the sex of a person, they are not considered a conversion practitioner. I don't get it. To me, it seems like hormonal and surgical intervention without professional diagnostic evaluation and differentiation is the ultimate conversion therapy.

Another paradox is thinking a newly transitioned person will no longer experience gender distress. If someone had a disorder related to body image, such as anorexia nervosa, medical professionals would not affirm the patient's distorted self-image by agreeing that the person was overweight when instead they were too thin. Yet for many families, a series of people, including medical professionals, suggest permanent surgical solutions to the many underlying issues their daughter or son was experiencing. I am confused as to why we don't help our young people accept their natural bodies and work through their bodily discomfort.

I am baffled by a recent internet search for "number of genders" available to choose from today. There are now over one hundred genders that one might self-identify with, and the list keeps growing. Some people flow from one identity to another as their feelings change. Who is creating this ever-expanding list, and is it really adding value to society?[10]

Another point that befuddles me seems to be the disagreement within the LGBTQ+ community about where to stop with all the letters. The lingo list keeps getting longer: LGBTQQIP2SA: Lesbian, Gay, Bisexual, Transgender, Queer, Questioning, Intersex, Pansexual, Two-Spirited, and Asexual.[11]

The LGB Alliance was formed in 2019 and registered as a charity in 2021. This alliance exists to provide support, advice, information, and community to men and women who are same-sex attracted. They advocate for same-sex rights and stand against all homophobia, including sex erasure.

In a YouTube interview, LGB Alliance co-founder Bev Jackson says that transgender ideology has caused a lot of tragedy for lesbians. She explains that LGB is about relationships, love, sex, and who you are attracted to. Whether someone is attracted to men, women, or both is a matter of sexual orientation. T and Q and all the other letters are about gender identity. Jackson said, "What we're seeing at the moment … hundreds of thousands of lesbians are having their breasts removed. It's no longer cool to be lesbian."[12,13,14]

Dr. Az Hakeem, a consultant psychiatrist in private practice, has explored therapy for people with gender dysphoria for over twenty years. He echoes the thought about the trend that being a lesbian is no longer cool. He has witnessed what he calls a fashionable subculture of trans and nonbinary identities from sites like Instagram and TikTok. He has found that, often, young women find that identifying as a trans male is more palatable than identifying as a lesbian. He reports that when he asks gender dysphoric girls if they know any lesbians, they don't. If he asks them if they know any trans men (biological women), they can recite loads of social influencers.

Ultimately, I hope to see more empowered lesbians become stronger role models for our young women to help offset this notion that lesbians are boring and not cool. I also hope that, as a society, we will accept and support gay leadership.

I am also perplexed about why gay and lesbian people are being targeted by the LGBTQ community. This trend has been given a name, and media outlets are picking up on it. *Newsweek* featured an article on April 21, 2022, entitled "The New Homophobia" by Ben Appel, who identifies as gay. He wrote,

"There is a frightening new version of homophobia pervading the US, disguised as, of all things, 'LGBTQ' activism. For adult gay people like me, it's clear that this activism does not advance our equality, but in fact compromises our ability to live peacefully in society. In fact, it is threatening our very existence."

Appel became an intern in 2017 with a major LGBTQ rights organization, but his excitement soon ebbed away. "I was, I quickly learned, not the right kind of 'queer.' I was just another 'cis' (short for 'cisgender,' a word I had never even heard until it was assigned to me, typically as a slur) gay male—in other words, a privileged and unevolved relic of the past. After all, I had my rights—the right to marry, the right to serve openly in the military, the right to assimilate into this oppressive, 'cisheteronormative,' patriarchal society. It was time to make way for a new generation of 'queer,' one that had very little to do with sex-based rights and more to do with abolishing the concepts of sex and sexuality altogether."

He expressed concern about this trend from the radical activists he once longed to emulate, those "who push a regressive, anti-liberal agenda that reifies gender stereotypes, downplays the seriousness of long-term medicalization and ultimately seeks to abolish my identity—for without biological sex, there is no homosexuality. Today, the least-accepting spaces for people like me are, of all places, the halls of LGBT rights organizations, where the threat might not be violence but is nevertheless terrible stigmatization and shame."[15]

Appel also wrote in *Spiked* on May 14, 2023, "For voicing my concerns about gender affirming care for minors, I have been called a transphobic bigot. If that's what speaking out against the medicalization of homosexuality makes me, then so be it."[16] I find Appel's account astonishing.

The ideological agenda of transgender movement has also upset transsexuals. One transsexual individual expressed, "The 'trans umbrella' may be multifaceted and vast, but the erasure of the transsexual narrative within it is glaring and detrimental ... Gender ideology erases our struggle just as it undermines what it means to be homosexual ... Every time 'trans' or 'transgender' is used interchangeably with 'transsexual,' this unwanted alliance is reinforced." — Tired Transsexual[17]

It may be new to readers, as it was for me, that there might be a difference between transsexuals and those participating in the new transgender movement. Some individuals undergo sexual reassignment surgery to function. A "Tired Transsexual" explains that "At its core, transsexualism, *as I understand and experience it*, is a medical condition that causes a person to reject their natal sex and feel a profound alignment with the opposite sex. This alignment permeates every facet of life: physically, psychologically, behaviorally, sexually, and even in terms of loyalty.

Whereas transsexualism for me is a deeply personal battle, transgenderism, from my observations, revolves around control and societal demands." Tired Transsexual also expressed that modern transgenderism often hinges on social validation, emphasized by pronoun usage and external recognition, and the "trans" narrative has strayed from the lived experience of transsexuals and morphed into an optional "gender journey" that one can choose.

Readers of my book might initially assume that I am against all sexual reassignment treatments and surgeries. Minors and individuals under the age of twenty-five should not have access to these medicalized choices because the brain is not considered fully developed until at least the mid-twenties.[18] Also, children need time to mature and understand the consequences of irreversible body damage and adverse health effects resulting from taking cross-sex hormones and having healthy body parts removed. I do not advocate the elimination of this option for those over age twenty-five, but extreme caution and due diligence of differential diagnoses and an exploration of natural alternatives need to be addressed first.

I suspect that people who blanketly proclaim they are pro-LGBTQ+ because it sounds like a nice social justice-minded thing to do may not have spent much time digging into what that actually means and how it harms so many facets of society and groups within it. If I didn't understand much of what was going on until I lost a daughter to a supposed progressive ideology, perhaps my readers are also mystified by what they hear in the news and what their daughter or son is talking about when they declare they are trans. Has anyone asked the child why they are denouncing their own sex and natural body? Could their wish or decision to transition stem from something such as a rebellion against sex stereotypes, the discomfort of same-sex attraction, desiring personal autonomy, or running from trauma, abuse, or loss? Might there be untreated or ineffectively treated mental issues or underlying commonalities? Could transition be a coping mechanism for deep pain?

Sometimes a decision to transition comes from a place of shame, such as when a young adult feels shame for their same-sex attraction, and the ability to transition gives them the idea that they can then have a relationship with the same gender and have it look straight. In other cases, it is the parents who feel the shame of having a gay kid and push for the transition so they feel better. Internal discomfort with same-sex attraction by the young adult or the parent is not an appropriate reason to undergo medicalization procedures.

Also, in some cases, parents are pushing medicalization to receive attention by showcasing their trans-identifying child. On the PBD Podcast hosted by Patrick Bet-David, an episode described parents who wish to display how "woke" and accepting they are within their political party. (Woke culture may be described as giving attention to issues related to racial and social injustice.) By encouraging their kids to transition to an appearance of the opposite sex and then parading that child around publicly, they wish to receive a badge of honor as progressive.[19]

These scenarios disturb me. If parents pushing cross-sex medicalization procedures are getting applause, and parents who exercise caution or do not want healthy body parts of their children removed are demonized, something is upside down. Can a rushed medicalization path sort out all the possibilities? Questions and confusion abound!

A rabbit hole that is not in the scope of this book to explore but nonetheless causes me confusion is hearing that some kids may be transitioning due to the discomfort of growing up in a privileged household. A girl who is white, smart, fit, and beautiful might feel shame about being in a category of white privilege. A white cisgendered person could be considered an oppressor, so some kids are identifying as trans, which places them in a powerless victim position to alleviate their shame. Arielle Scarcella, who identifies as gay, is an outspoken critic of trans ideology. In the YouTube channel *Triggernometry*, hosts Konstantin Kisin and Francis Foster interview Scarcella in an episode entitled *"Trans Ideology Is Homophobia": Lesbian Speaks Out*. Scarcella discussed how woke culture looks at cis and straight people as the bottom of the pole when it comes to respect. She mentioned that you can get "oppression points" if, as a white straight or gay person, you identify as trans.[20]

Helena Kirschner, who identified as a trans man when she was eighteen, echoes that ideas spread through the internet about so-called privilege, being white and heterosexual, create a sense of shame among some young people, and they begin to despise what they perceive makes them "privileged." In *Lost in Trans Nation* by Dr. Miriam Grossman, Kirschner is quoted as saying, "They can't change their sexual orientation or race. But they can change their gender. Transgenderism offers a way for adolescents to be absolved of privilege and join the ranks of the oppressed."[21]

It is valid that my daughter and many other daughters do not fit into traditional female stereotypes and wish to break off from what they perceive as a box in which they do not fit. Most parents I know are fairly relaxed about clothing and hairstyles but balk at cutting off healthy breasts and other medicalized procedures as a countercultural statement. We have also observed social media posts in which former women, now living as men, are fighting their perception of patriarchy by defining a "new masculinity." Will this drastic display and life change be effective in changing public mindsets, or will it worsen the problems they wish to address? If a kid purposely becomes part of a marginalized or victim group to feel less shame and seem heroic, we must examine this motive.

Where did these concepts come from? "The Wheel of Privilege" is being taught in some schools now.[22] James Esses explains that "this type of narrative only further propagates a culture of victimhood in our society. Far from instilling a sense of resiliency in our children, which is crucial in a world that is often unpredictable and unfair, it tells whole swathes that they are victims because of certain characteristics they possess, and that they will, to some extent, always remain victims. This takes away any incentive or motivation to work to make your life a success, particularly when it pays to be seen as a victim in modern society."

Is your head spinning yet? Someone identifying as transgender can have numerous and complex reasons for their transition. Outsiders who observe social media posts of women who are transitioning or have transitioned to present as trans men report that the transitioners say they are defying stereotypes and redefining masculinity. Their transition seems calculated and agenda-based. Does that agenda make surgery appropriate? Do affirmation-only advocates understand all the nuances of this ideology? How can parents of a newly trans-identified child make sense of all this information? And why do others suggest parents support their child's transition without question?

Taking testosterone via a syringe injection to the thigh, or other methods of application, seems to be all the rage right now. I can appreciate that the allure of the initial increased energy and reduction in symptoms for those suffering from depression must be very appealing to young women at first. Doctors who treat detransitioners have noticed that sometimes women experience a pre-surgery euphoria (before a mastectomy, for example), but later regret appears. The issues they had hoped would go away did not disappear, such as their feelings of not fitting in. Those who prescribe testosterone seem to downplay the horrible consequences that can occur over time to women. I am baffled that clinics and doctors are prescribing testosterone without warning kids of the potential long-term effects of dependency on this drug. Could they have an alliance with a pharmaceutical drug company? Are they interested in financial profit by creating drug and medical dependency in young people?

Sinéad Watson, a Scottish woman, medically transitioned as an adult between 2015 and 2019. She began to detransition in October 2019. Ever since, she has been speaking out for those who suffer from gender dysphoria and those who regret transitioning.

Watson shared her story in an interview in 2022 at the LGB Alliance Conference, and the video is posted on YouTube. Excerpts from the interview include:

> "All the problems I was running from with transition were still there."

> "I didn't need hormones and surgery; I needed therapy."

> "Changing your body doesn't address the mental distress you're feeling."

> "If you really truly think that transitioning and changing yourself and taking cross-sex hormones and surgeries, which have a whole lane of risks with them, is going to make you mentally happy, you're deluding yourself, and it's cruel."

> "I wish it was reversible. I wish I could have my voice back; I wish I could feel my chest; I wish that I didn't have bladder problems; I wish that everything transition did to me was reversible, but I am living proof that that is not true."[23]

When a young girl or woman decides to take testosterone, she is committing to relying on a prescription drug and constant injections of that drug for the rest of her life instead of letting the body's natural hormones perform their job with no pharmaceutical intervention. All the cells and organs in a female body have XX chromosomal coding within them. The body has a delicate balance that is disturbed by the cross-sex hormone of testosterone.

I am puzzled about why this drug dependency and its adverse effects are minimized or not discussed before a young person begins the trans train trajectory.

I am baffled about all the ever-expanding and changing new words I am told I must learn. Many glossaries are available to help people understand the vocabulary. The lists change frequently. If I included a current, comprehensive list in this book, it would probably be outdated the week after publication, so it is best to look up the list on the internet for the latest version.

I am told I am not just a woman anymore; I am a "cis woman," which is a person who identifies as a woman, presents herself as feminine, and is biologically female. Parents of transitioning daughters may have been given a list of forbidden words, many of which are very endearing to them: daughter, sister, girl, she, and her. Instead, they must say child or kid, sibling, and gender-neutral or opposite-sex pronouns for their daughters.

Many young people say they are queer and have embraced queer theory. When I was growing up, the word "queer" was a derogatory slur against gay people. Times have changed, and the word has been reclaimed. According to Wikipedia:

> ***Queer*** *is an umbrella term for people who are not heterosexual or are not cisgender. Originally meaning 'strange' or 'peculiar,' queer came to be used pejoratively against those with same-sex desires or relationships in the late 19th century. Beginning in the late 1980s, queer activists, such as the members of Queer Nation, began to reclaim the word as a deliberately provocative and politically radical alternative to the more assimilationist branches of the LGBT community.*[24]

I looked up the term "queer theory," and I struggled to find a description I could present here. The language was challenging to interpret. Here is an excerpt of how this theory is presented by Illinois Library:

> *Queer theory's origin is hard to clearly define, since it came from multiple critical and cultural contexts, including feminism, post-structuralist theory, radical movements of people of color, the gay and lesbian movements, AIDS activism, many sexual subcultural practices such as sadomasochism, and postcolonialism.*
>
> *Queer theory as an academic tool came about in part from gender and sexuality studies that in turn had their origins from lesbians and gay studies and feminist theory. It is a much newer theory, in that it was established in the 1990s, and contests many of the set ideas of the more established fields it comes from by challenging the notion of defined and finite identity*

> *categories, as well as the norms that create a binary of good versus bad sexualities. Queer theorists' contention is that there is no set normal, only changing norms that people may or may not fit into, making queer theorists' main challenge to disrupt binaries in hopes that this will destroy difference as well as inequality.*[25]

I have no desire to argue about this theory, but it seems from what I have read that proponents of the theory desire to upend conventional thinking, postulating that sex is not innate but rather socially constructed. Also, queer theory advocates seem to want to erase sex categories. They also like to rewrite history. Any woman in the past who did not follow a female stereotype must have been a trans man. Joan of Arc or Jo of *Little Women* are now relabeled as trans men by the queer movement. Butch lesbians might also be lumped into this new narrative too. Oddly, the desire to erase men doesn't seem to measure up to the thrust to eliminate women.

I am also puzzled about the gender concept of fluid, which can apparently change all the time. What is gender fluid? According to WebMD:

> *Someone who is fluid—also called gender fluid—is a person whose gender identity (the gender they identify with most) is not fixed. It can change over time or from day to day. Fluid is a form of gender identity or gender expression, rather than a sexual orientation.*
>
> *Fluid relates to how a person identifies themselves internally and presents themselves to the world. A person who is gender fluid may identify as male one day, female the next, both male*

and female, or neither. It affects their gender expression—the way a person presents themself to society (masculine, feminine, both, or neither).

People who are fluid don't abide by societal norms and expectations that classify people within a binary (either male or female; either masculine or feminine). The term "genderqueer" might also be used to describe a person who is fluid. Genderqueer describes someone whose gender identity doesn't fit within the binary.

Other LGBT+ terms for fluid include agender (no gender), bigender (both male and female), demigender (partial connection to a certain gender), or another nonbinary identity.

Instead of using binary-restricted pronouns, such as "his/him/he" and "her/she/hers," a person who is gender fluid may use the more neutral terms "they/them/their" instead.[26]

Another example of new vocabulary is the proclamation that one can be triple gender. Trigender or triple gender is a polygender identity in which a person shifts between three genders. This experience may be simultaneous or fluid. The individual shifts between male, female, and a non-binary gender.[27]

My question is that if someone believes they can be fluid, why cut off healthy body parts if their gender is likely to flow from one sex to another or neither? Why not explore gender stereotypes without entering a permanent medical pathway of drugs and surgery? I can imagine it could be intoxicating to turn stereotypes and social systems upside down, but that may not be the right reason to transition.

If I am confused, then someone who identifies as trans could also be confused. As I searched for clarity about the trans movement, I found a site, Post Trans, which is a collection of detrans stories from female detransitioners and desisters.[28]

On the Post Trans website, you will find a free, downloadable booklet entitled *Gender Detransition: a path towards self-acceptance.* Many stories are available to read on the site as well. I have included a few excerpts here as an example of the experiences that are shared by detransitioners and desisters. Because I suspect that many young women are not comfortable in their own bodies and perhaps are not fully self-accepting of being a lesbian, discussions of that view caught my eye when I read the accounts.

> *I felt like I was too ugly and socially awkward to ever be a female. I thought that me being a female was a disgusting thing and I was so ashamed of it. Transition was a way to escape that shame. I was more attractive as a male, and I felt less disgusted by my attraction to women. Me being male made sense in a way—I had masculine interests, I looked masculine, I was attracted to women ... I wish I could say detransition made me feel better but it really didn't. I feel ashamed of what I did. I feel like I completely destroyed my own body ... I ruined all the relationships that I had because I truly thought transitioning would make me happy, would make me right, and everyone who got in the way of that was also getting in the way of happiness so I had to cut them out. The worst part is that I did this to myself. I don't have anyone else to blame. And that is really hard to live with.*[29]

> *I learned that being transgender stemmed from hating the way I was perceived in society and being so deeply immersed in the*

lgbt community that I thought the only way to be a masculine lesbian was to be a trans man.[30]

Transition was a means of escape ... I know now I'm simply a butch lesbian. I feel at home with myself, and have begun repairing my relationship with my body. I thought for so long we were two separate things, but now I know my body is actively me, and I am not an outsider in it. ... Detransition was a shock in my system that woke me up from a fantasy, and I couldn't be more thankful I found the community of detransitioned women online.[31]

The main reason why I started to physically transition was the strong disgust and disconnection I felt towards my body. Testosterone treatment seemed like the only solution to make it better ... I never understood why I started to suddenly hate my body so much. I thought it was simply because I was trans and that this dysphoria would go away with HRT. And it did. The price for it was to live socially as a man and to give up on my lesbian identity ... So I lied to therapists, I lied to doctors, to my family and friends in order to have access to what looked like the only solution for me. I eventually started to lie to myself.*[32]

(*HRT: Hormone Replacement Therapy)

These frank and candid expressions of regret from brave women are worth contemplating. The Reddit detrans community was over fifty thousand members at the time of this publication, and numbers are rising steadily. The more I learned, the more the trans community and their aligned media outlets' dismissal of these courageous people seemed inappropriate. At that point, I began moving from confusion to concern.[33]

A Parent's Concern

AS A MOM, I AM PRONE TO WORRY about my daughter (even though she is an adult now) and young girls overall when it comes to the trend of self-identification to the opposite sex, believing they were born into the wrong body, and the decision to engage in medical intervention to fix their perceived body mismatch with cross-sex hormones and surgery. I and many other parents feel uneasy when girls and young women do not give themselves time to sort out all their hurts and confusion. Parents are anxious that when our children are most vulnerable, they are giving power to a group that doesn't really know them. Kids grab onto an influencer's quick-fix idea without fully understanding the risks and far-reaching consequences of permanently altering their body and their health.

I accepted my daughter being gay. I became skeptical when she moved into a nonbinary presentation, although I could understand that she might not wish to be a stereotypical female. I became doubtful when she moved over into zeal to present herself as a trans man, rejecting her natural body.

Girls caught up in the trans culture likely have a complex history, often involving trauma and issues that professionals and psychiatrists are more qualified to diagnose and treat than social media influencers, who might downplay or disregard serious underlying conditions. Mastectomies are rarely lifesaving for a newly trans-identifying girl; the surgery is often enabling body self-loathing. When parents see social media comments that debase body parts, it indicates a lack of honor for one's natural body. Social media influencers who glamorize, glorify, or make false promises to vulnerable youth are inappropriate and move into the territory of unethical.

Parents are concerned about what is being taught in our schools. School curricula is being radically changed. Kindergartners are now taught about a Genderbread Person and Gender Unicorn. Feelings usurp biology in education in the new narrative. Kids are given a multitude of gender possibilities that they might be and are asked to feel into one. They are pressed to pick one, even if they are uncomfortable or confused. More and more, identifying with one's natal sex is uncool. Children might hear teachers say how brave a child is when they pick an option different from their biological sex. "Cis kids" may be shamed for claiming their natal sex and may adopt a false identity to avoid criticism.

Perhaps schools originally had good intentions of inclusivity and reducing bullying by teaching kids as young as kindergarten about the Genderbread Person, but has it gone too far? Have they put more focus on sex and the body than kids really need or can handle? When a kid gets indoctrinated young and then peer pressure and social media influences add on to the body, sex, and gender focus, it seems like the perfect environment for children to show signs of body discomfort and gender confusion.

Parents of teens and young adults often report their child seems self-absorbed, spending a lot of time in front of the mirror, fixated on their body and hair. This body fixation may extend into provocative poses that they photograph. One only needs to scan Instagram and type in key word searches such as transgender to see many selfies; some are cringe-worthy or disturbing. Why does this group spend so much time focusing on their bodies and gender issues instead of life outside of themselves? Are schools inadvertently participating in this trend of body focus?

I would not want to be a mother of a pre-teen or teen in today's world. When my girls were that age, they went to a girls' summer camp. Now camps are starting to allow boys who self-ID as girls into sleeping quarters and showering areas with girls. This inclusion could infringe upon the privacy and safety of girls. Is it appropriate for boys to get free entry into all-girl spaces if they feel like a girl or like girl activities? Perhaps a better alternative would be to have trans camps or sessions for trans-identifying kids within the calendar of choices so that each can have separation.

Being a long-term patient in the medical system starting at a young age is not something one generally wants to volunteer for or aspire to. Parents throughout the world are concerned that strangers are swaying their kids to listen to them, or their kids are swayed by their friends who also listened to strangers instead of relying on their parents' love and wisdom. Parents are disturbed when social media influencers are focused on getting more fame, followers, likes, and comments as they convince vulnerable young people to do drastic things to themselves.

Parents are concerned about the safety of young girls as they jump on board this alarming trend. We cannot imagine how they will ever feel at home or be safe in a men's restroom or locker room. How will they interact with the guys at the urinals or in the shower area? We are apprehensive that natural-born men will ever really accept trans men (biological women) into their domain. Could these women, attempting to pass as men, be attacked in their spaces?

Some media outlets trouble moms and dads as well. Captured media showcases heartwarming stories about kids declaring their cross-sex identities, with parents who jump into the new activist movement with their kids without question. Media outlets that adopt the transgender agenda ignore detransitioners, saying they are rare. The same media outlets that align with gender as a social construct point fingers at parents who disagree, joining the kids in saying we are ignorant, negligent, and abusive people. This viewpoint seems to miss the complexity and the controversy of transgender ideology.

We are worried that the young athletes who were females originally but transitioned to presenting as males will never be able to play on a woman's sports team again or be able to enjoy the camaraderie of strong, sporty women. Moms, in particular, are distressed when thinking about all the wonderful women's organizations of all kinds that their daughters will never have the opportunity to engage in.

There is concern that some women are discarding their membership within the lesbian group and that their dating pool will shrink. If a young-woman-turned-trans-man is attracted to other women, those other women may reject them, wishing instead for their potential partner to have a woman's body, including breasts. It is troubling to hear reports of a lack of sexual pleasure and a prevalence of sexual dysfunction among women who medically made themselves into presenting as trans men. Trans-identifying people have selected a tiny group in which to search for a relationship. One day, it may hit them hard when they realize all they have lost.

As trans inclusivity creeps into dating sites, it affects non-trans-identifying single people too. Not all dating apps are transparent, and a dating profile may not include natal sex, which can lead to surprises later in the get-acquainted stage. Can we trust anyone to be honest about their sex anymore?

Young women transitioners may be able to pass as a man, but their XX chromosomes will always remain XX. Biological sex and feminine essence are usually picked up by others' subconscious minds, and so it is possible that they will be misgendered for years to come, which might be painful or tiring. A gentle reminder to those identifying as trans men that you are a female having a female experience of not liking your breasts. You have the autonomy to cut them off your body, but a mastectomy does not make you a man; this act is not a male experience. Women may have both a mastectomy and a hysterectomy, which makes them females without breasts and without reproductive systems, but these drastic surgeries do not make females become males.

As a result of not being able to change their innate biology, women presenting as trans men will face battles every day as they artificially and synthetically try to present as a man to the world. Parents feel anxious and sad to think that, at some point, the fight with nature might become exhausting or that complications, misgendering, and regret might overwhelm them and diminish their health and well-being.

On a detransition platform, an anonymous girl said, "Life does not feel worth living after mastectomy. I'm nothing without my breasts. My thick beautiful hair is gone, my face is changed, but all that I could deal with if only I wasn't in constant pain from the surgery. I would give anything to be whole. I've been contemplating suicide for months now. I basically already killed myself, destroyed the person I was at the ripe old age of 20. It's been three years since the surgery and I still hurt every minute, the scars are so tight and I'm always in sensory overload. I won't even be able to have a good career because of my appearance, I am too broken to have the family I tried to pretend I didn't want when I was transitioning. My life is a dead end. Do I really want to spend the next sixty years working retail and wallowing in regret? I can't believe I did this. Sometimes it feels like I'll wake up and this will all have been a nightmare. But I never wake up. It just keeps going. I'm in so much pain and I just want it to end."

Some girls are blessed (and maybe cursed, too) with having above-average beauty according to current beauty standards; they became gorgeous young women in their teens and twenties. They may have had difficulty handling their beauty as a woman. It may have brought them unwanted attention. Good looks may have caused advances from men, which they did not welcome, particularly if the young woman identified as gay. One way to stop all that unwanted attention is to remove outward signs of femininity. The possible reasons for transitioning are complex and vast, and the harm to children is becoming clear, which begs the question of why affirmation-only for self-ID of trans is ever a wise choice.

Parents are bothered when we hear others spinning words to make this drastic decision sound easy or happy. Hormone therapy for kids and young adults is actually the prescription for a lifelong drug dependency. It is a disservice to kids when people, especially in the medical community, use terminology that minimizes radical surgery. Top surgery is a double mastectomy. Bottom surgery can include the removal of the ovaries, uterus, and vagina in women and the penis and scrotum in men. Additional surgeries may also occur in an attempt to create a penis for a woman after her hysterectomy. Say it like it is and use appropriate medical terminology.

Who really has these young women's backs? Their new trans community friends have only been in their lives for a very short time. Some are strangers, such as online influencers, and are not their friends at all. They are a powerful group because they convince vulnerable people to discard their families and their healthy body parts. Their power to extinguish a girl's ability to see her own light and her body's natural beauty is astonishing. Will that community be there for them if they have doubts or regrets or get off the trans train? Based on my reading and viewing of the testimonies of detransitioners and desisters, those who change course and return to being a woman will be ostracized, admonished, and abandoned. Transgender activists' community disdain for anyone who leaves their fold can be vicious and cruel. Most desisting/detransitioning kids and parents are so worn down by this ruthless treatment of their lives, health, and relationships that they go into hiding for safety and to heal.

Thousands of parents have been discarded by trans-identifying kids. Helen Joyce, in her book *Trans*, clarifies the reason this often happens. "The categories of man and woman underpin those of father and mother, and the relationship of each of their children. If such categories are to become a matter of self-declaration, then those ties must be dissolved. Families become meaningless and individuals create themselves."

Families that believe in a biological base of sex and question their children's self-diagnosis and feelings of being in the wrong body are likely to be excised from their kid's life. They are usually renamed the "bio family." A parent's concern for their kid's physical health, emotional and mental well-being, and their safety and future in the world are often scoffed at. Parents are no longer relevant in the new gender ideological narrative where kids may declare their own reality and parents must bend to that reality.

If these young adults encounter problems in their lives and need help or want to get off the trans train and find support to detransition, who will be their backup? It can be challenging to revive and repair a damaged relationship with parents and family. What if kids who identify as trans wait too long to value their parents again? What if a parent or grandparent dies before they want to work to rebuild the relationships they once had with one another? Will they be able to live with the regret and guilt that might surface in the face of that loss? Will they be able to handle the remorse?

I have a coffee-table picture book entitled *Wise Women: A Celebration of Their Insights, Courage, and Beauty*. My dad gave me the book and inscribed it, "To Lisa, I am so proud to be your Dad. Feb. '07." My dad gifted me that book for my birthday, and I am grateful that he honored women. The book is filled with pictures of middle-aged and older women, and quotes accompany the photographs. The author and creator of the book, Joyce Tenneson, wrote the following as her dedication: "I dedicate this book to all the extraordinary women in these pages who entrusted me with their faces, their bodies, their thoughts. I admire their courage, their wit, their strength, and their beauty. They are the true revealers of the inner power of wise women in our time." I feel concerned to my core for trans-identifying kids who lose the chance to mature and become wise women.

Recently, a photo circulated on Facebook showing fifteen women of all body sizes and breast sizes posing in the nude by a tree. It was an honoring photograph that seemed to say, "Women are beautiful." It's hard to imagine a positive reaction of viewers to fifteen young girls and women with flattened chests and mastectomy scars, all resembling each other as breastless, replacing those natural women. The spectacle of kids flaunting their mastectomies also dishonors women who lost their breasts to cancer and grieve that loss.

Chloe Cole, a detransitioner, said on a Twitter post, "The scar worship was one of the first things I saw when I got into the trans cult. Most girls that go through this have significant sexual trauma around their chest." Might the investigation and treatment of trauma be an appropriate first measure before scheduling a mastectomy? How did our society and medical model evolve into one that celebrates the removal of healthy breasts as progressive? Why are kids turning against themselves and their natural bodies? When our youth harm themselves and refer to their natural bodies in derogatory ways, we must seriously evaluate their influences and mindsets. Why are we not asking hard questions about this mastectomy trend?

Question upon question arises for silenced parents of kids who identify as trans, such as, "Whoever came up with the idea that a kid should take drugs to be their true, authentic self?" Just because trans-presenting kids seem to loathe their natural bodies and perhaps feel discomfort that they are gay doesn't mean it is appropriate to enable permanent, radical mastectomy surgery. Treatment of trauma, underlying conditions, and mental issues takes time. Social media influencers grab onto hurting kids with the promise of quick-fix happiness that cross-sex hormones may initially give. That sounds like a drug dealer's philosophy of hooking young people into customers for a lifelong drug dependency. What parent would not be troubled by this ideological movement?

Many grandparents of kids who identify as trans are devastated by the loss of their beloved grandchildren. Some of these grandparents will never see their granddaughter or grandson again, and if they do, the grandchild is often unrecognizable, and relations become strained. The ripple effect and agony of loss within families are profound.

Concerns continue begging the question: "Whatever happened to valuing a doctor or a therapist who digs deep to uncover the whole person instead of just one dimension of their feelings about gender?" Young people getting pulled into the medicalized trans train are often intelligent kids who are not afraid to bend the truth or minimize issues of the past to get their testosterone prescriptions and surgeries scheduled. Gender affirming practitioners either do not see this deceit, do not recognize the use of a practiced script (possibly one found online), or are not allowed to ask questions other than maybe one, "Are you sure?" which is always answered as "Yes" by a youth who wants a quick, feel-better-now solution to their discomforts.

Do educators or counselors consider the whole family as well? Mothers are rarely asked for their thoughts on their daughters' lives. I certainly was not asked by any doctor or professional. In my case, I was the one who watched every year of my daughter's twenty-eight years of life unfold, but I was canceled from participating in her life-altering decision by strangers who hadn't set foot in our home or ever talked with me. How do people develop such arrogance, casting parents as subservient or inconsequential, in brief conversations with a young person? Any parent who does not agree with and affirm their child's feelings and radical interventions becomes the enemy of the school and the child. How did our society evolve to debase and exclude parents?

One answer is ideological capture, which is when an ideological group takes over an institution and redirects the goals, mission, and resources of that institution toward serving the interests of the ideological group. Sadly, many of our school leaders and medical field professionals have been captured.[34]

Despite this capture, we need to return to valuing therapy to explore the big picture of thoughts, feelings, motivations, past traumas, and mental conditions that a person may need to heal or receive further specific care for. Parents in the support groups in which I belong talk about the issues their kids had prior to them self-diagnosing and announcing they were trans. Commonalities reported are depression, anxiety, autism spectrum disorder, eating disorders, and more.

Susan Bradley, a Canadian psychiatrist, discusses that many trans identifications are occurring in kids on the autism spectrum. She discusses that "If such children prefer clothing or activities associated with the opposite sex, or are experiencing the early stirrings of same-sex attraction, they may conclude that they have been misclassified. Also common in people with autistic traits is lack of insight into one's feelings, in particular low self-esteem caused by perceived rejection by peers. Such children may latch onto a concrete explanation for their misery: that they were 'born in the wrong body.'"

In an article entitled "Understanding Vulnerability in Girls and Young Women with High-Functioning Autism Spectrum Disorder," Bradley highlights:

- Clinically, the parents of these girls regularly speak of their daughters' difficulties regulating their feelings.
- Developmentally, these young girls have typically had trouble making friends and often feel rejected and left out of peer groups.
- They often think of themselves as different in some way that they find hard to explain.
- Crushes on popular girls are not uncommon in many teens, but not knowing this, the emotions that are aroused may make these young women feel increasingly "weird." In the current culture of politically correct affirmation of gender dysphoria, it translates into meaning that you are "trans," which, for many young women, is less anxiety-provoking than being lesbian.
- Being welcomed by "trans" advocates acts as the external push.[35]

Some kids are undiagnosed but express autistic traits. If these kids get love-bombed by online trans influencers, they might misattribute their discomforts with trans and not seek effective solutions to their social and cognitive issues. Might a practitioner or therapist who counsels gender dysphoric or trans-identifying girls want to explore this information before engaging in an affirmation-only stance?

We need to engage with the family for deeper insight into the dysfunctions and dynamics that led to a decision to make permanent body changes with surgery. Taking the easy route of writing a prescription for testosterone after one or two short visits, instead of careful evaluation and exploration, is woefully inadequate.

It is troubling to see the viciousness of the trans activist community. Dr. Az Hakeem is a consultant psychiatrist, medical psychotherapist, and a Fellow of the Royal College of Psychiatrists. Since he has spoken out on his concerns about the transgender movement, he has been the recipient of critical backlash from trans activists. He wrote:

> *"Hostility has also come from the trans activists—or the trans-terrorists, as I tend to call them. This is a term I use because the aim of the trans-terrorists is to instill fear and ruin the lives of those who do not fit in with their manifesto and ideals. These are people who have never seen me in a professional capacity, indeed my patients have always found me to be quite open minded, quite thoughtful and quite caring and non-judgmental. The trans-terrorists direct their vitriol towards me because of what they think I represent rather than the actuality. I had the accolade of being referred to as "the most*

evil dangerous Nazi Psychiatrist in the world" by one particular excitable trans-terrorist. This person has never met me but was reacting to the fact that I was offering psychotherapy for gender dysphoria rather than hormones and surgery. They presumed I was offering some form of conversion therapy, whereas in actual fact all I offer is a neutral exploratory space in which a person can think about their gender confusion without being convinced to do something or not to do something."[36]

A few years ago, a disturbing message by the group identifying as #PrideTrain emerged in signs posted in subway stations in New York City, saying, "Respect trans people or your pronouns will be was/were." The NYC transportation organization said it did not put up the signs and it would remove them from transit stations. This radical declaration should alert everyone to the magnitude of the threats being made by trans extremists.

The minimization of the risks of removing healthy breast tissue contributes to the lack of true informed consent of minors undergoing irreversible surgeries. In a mastectomy procedure, complications might include bleeding, infection, poor healing of incisions, hematoma, loss of nipple sensation, loss of the nipple and areola, pain, and anesthesia risks. Breasts can't grow back, and if you later decide you wish to nurse a baby, you will not be able to. At the time of the publication of this book, the procedure ranges from $6,000 to $10,000 USD. This may or may not include consultation fees, hidden fees, and medical supplies. In some states and countries, taxpayers are funding the surgeries. In other cases, kids create a GoFundMe account to raise money for the surgery if their parents' insurance policy doesn't cover it, if the parent removes the child from their policy, or they have aged out of inclusion. Furthermore, Planned Parenthood clinics in the US are giving cross-sex hormones to anyone over the age of eighteen who asks for them. Is that a wise use of their funds and resources? Wouldn't it be a wonderful pivot if all this money wasn't padding the pockets of clinics and unethical surgeons? Wouldn't it be refreshing if resources were instead funneled into taking a full history and treating the whole child, including underlying issues?[37]

The list of concerns mounts as bystanders outside of the parent group begin to see the progression of gender identity ideology as it infiltrates feminine terminology, female spaces, and women's rights.

It begins with young girls and women disowning feminine pronouns and birth names, but it can progress quickly to disgust of their own breasts. Self-loathing of that representation of being a woman leads to binding, which is painful and harmful to the body. Constant discomfort and pain from compression of the breasts can lead to further disdain of them and a plan for their removal with a mastectomy. One only needs to type in "Top Surgery" into a YouTube search to see the proud display of the mastectomy chests and scars and see their celebration of ridding themselves of their perceived useless body part.

Gender identity ideology seems to dehumanize women and divide them up into bodily secretions and bodily organs to be inclusive of trans-presenting people. Examples:

- People who menstruate or bleed or menstruators, also known as bleeders and breeders

- Vagina owners (vagina may also be renamed as a front hole or bonus hole)
- Uterus havers
- Ovary havers
- Non-prostate owners
- Child bearers
- Birthing bodies
- Human milk or chest feeders
- Elimination of the word "mother" in maternity policies
- Elimination of the word "woman" in cervical screening/pap test literature

Note: The word *man* has not been eliminated from prostate screening literature. Why must women relinquish the words *woman* and *mother*, yet men get to keep the word *man*? One reason for the language change is to avoid offending those who identify as nonbinary, but only biological women have female reproductive organs, and only mothers have birthing experiences. And let's also be clear that "trans women" (biological men) will never menstruate, have a uterus, get pregnant, or experience giving birth or breastfeeding a child. The betrayal and erasure of women and mothers is unacceptable.

Many people feel alarmed at the derogation of women and motherhood. But none of that is enough for the extreme transgender activist. Societal spaces and sanctuaries for females are being threatened with being disassembled if they do not allow admittance of trans women (biological men). Women's sports are being infiltrated with men who wish to be women, destroying the fairness of competition. Trans activists want women's restrooms and locker rooms to allow men who identify as women, as well. Men must allow women, newly identifying as trans men, in their restrooms too. Complimentary menstrual products are now found in many men's restrooms with signs that say, "People of all genders menstruate, and we are committed to creating inclusive spaces where people can use the restroom consistent with their gender identity and have access to necessary products." The new trans man (biological woman) seems to have abandoned women, lesbians, and matriarchy. Who is left to advocate for women's rights, safeguard women's spaces, and create women's leadership?

When trans groups and individuals adopt critical theories aimed at dismantling traditional models of society, organizations, and the family unit, they may not realize that they are destroying the good parts and the good people within them. It is troublesome to observe trans-identifying kids cheer each other on with countdowns to surgery dates. Few express empathy when family relationships fray and unravel. Will they celebrate years down the road when they need their mom or family or want a sacred space that they destroyed?

The trans agenda also seems to wish to rewrite the history of strong women who broke barriers. It is alarming to read the trans narrative that says women who stepped out of gender-conforming roles were not actually brave, heroic women who expanded women's roles and rights but were actually men. Lesbian women leaders are particularly hit hard because they are being lumped into this narrative as well. Be discerning and careful of "trans-washing," the historical revision of individuals or organizations as "trans" when, in reality, the person may have been lesbian or gay and the group may have been fighting for gay rights. Trans-washing erases the truth.

Progress of the women's rights movement is being undermined by this history distortion. Remind me again, as a mom and woman, why I should be enthusiastic and supportive of trans ideology. I lost my daughter to it, and I am witnessing the conversion of girls and young women who express non-conforming female stereotypes to be medicalized to look like boys and men. We need those amazing girls and women as females, not trans men, to advocate for women's rights for themselves and others.

The list of concerns that transgender ideology brings to families and society seems to go on and on! Let's touch on another rabbit hole: drag shows. Many people, including transsexuals, have a problem with drag shows. "Tired Transsexual" wrote, "Drag parades hypersexualized, cartoonish stereotypes of femininity, playing into every misogynistic fantasy that women have fought. Drag queens revel in the caricatured extremes of womanhood, and then they go back to a life of male privilege. Drag is to transsexuals what minstrel shows were to black people. Society lauds drag artists with praise and Netflix specials while gleefully erasing the torment and plight of transsexuals. Keep clapping for the caricatures; just know you're part of the problem." Might readers reevaluate supporting drag shows or "Drag Queen Reading Hour" at your local library or school?

A hot button in trans discussion is cropping up, and it is that transgender ideology seems cult-like. Proponents of this concern identify cult characteristics that fit with trans ideology:

- Opposes critical thinking
- Requires unwavering devotion to a belief system and practices
- Love-bombs kids initially and welcomes them to the new group

- Isolates and manipulates members and encourages estrangement from family, suggesting they renounce and sever ties with anyone who doesn't adopt their new belief system
- Provides a surrogate family
- Exploits and damages the physical body and the mental health of its members
- Creates dependency
- Cultivates self-centered leadership and narcissistic behaviors of members as they interface with outsiders and non-affirming family
- Engages in gaslighting and rewriting history ("gaslighting" means to manipulate someone using psychological methods into questioning their own sanity or powers of reasoning)
- Financial exploitation

It seems that kids are susceptible to victimization when they have a trauma history, have been bullied, are on the autistic spectrum, are socially awkward, feel like a misfit, are same-sex attracted, or are experiencing emotional distress. Identifying as trans might give them temporary belonging and attention, but that does not mean it is a sound decision.

At this point in reading the book, your head might be exploding with growing awareness of the reach that transgender or gender identity ideology encompasses. Before exhaustion and overwhelm force you to put down the book and reevaluate all you thought and believed about "trans," let's ask a few more questions before we wrap up the Concern chapter.

Since there are stages of cross-sex transition, what makes one eligible to walk into a women's restroom, locker room, or spa? How can we maintain single-sex spaces for safety and privacy?

How many years or at what level do cross-sex hormones need to be in the body to be deemed eligible to compete in sports as the opposite sex? Who decides those questions? At what age did the competitor start hormones? Did they go through puberty? Have they had surgery? Who verifies what sex they are and by what measure or exam? How can the Olympics or any sports competition manage all the variables to decide who is eligible and who is not in regard to sex classification?

Might there be future issues—legally, medically, or otherwise—if someone changes their birth certificate to erase their natal sex and instead lists their gender preference? At what stage of transition can one change all their legal documents? Who makes the decision that documents can be altered? When a girl wishes she was born a boy, it does not make it so, yet she seems to be allowed to rewrite history and change the facts at a whim and without parental agreement. Why do we allow this revision of historical records?

The chaos, oversight, and minimization of the big picture of what is behind gender identity ideology feel unconscionable and lead parents from concern into anger.

A Parent's Anger

I SPEAK FOR MYSELF, and I speak for the many families suffering daily agony in the loss of their teens and young adult children. Callous cruelty abounds within the "affirmation-only" crowd. I am angry when I hear that another parent was asked, "Would you rather have a live trans child or a dead child?" or "Would you rather plan a transition or plan a funeral?" I find these questions completely inappropriate, and I am disturbed by the questioner's lack of evidence as well as empathy for the feelings of a caring parent.

Those who suggest that not immediately affirming trans self-identification will lead to suicide may not have investigated the mental health of individuals after transitioning. An anonymous detransitioner wrote this sentiment on a detransition platform: "Being trans is the most selfish thing you could ever do to your friends and family, and I regret forcing them into my delusions more than anything. I made them pretend like I was passing … I forced them to take a side in a political issue … I hate what I have done to myself and my family." The end of their post included a suicide intention. Is it not time to listen to detransitioners instead of minimizing them? Is it not time to study the long-term well-being of transitioners after their medical interventions? No parent should be threatened with suicide scare tactics.

Parents are told to "go get help" by their kids and by those who advocate a response of "affirmation-only" to their child's announcement of being trans. They seem to believe that an indication of successful therapy is for us to become educated, as if our impulse to question and express concern would be eliminated with the proper education. After we were rid of our ignorance, the next step would be to accept the belief system that our daughter or son was born into the wrong body. We would then need to celebrate the medicalized salvation solution that our kids chose with the help of social media videos and the gender affirmation care model. Only after we have succumbed to their demands to use new names and pronouns and adjust our use of language to their new rules will we be held in good standing and allowed to remain in their lives. We might get extra credit if we can see beauty in their mastectomy scars. Until that time, we are expected to keep up with therapy or get a better or different therapist. If parents cannot achieve agreement with their child's new feelings regarding themselves, then the parents will be excised from their kid's life and considered a sad case of obsolescence.

I love and cherish my daughter. I have been an "all-in" mom every step of the way until I was shut out for expressing concern about a surgical remedy to complex issues. I have been present for all her special milestone events and celebrated with her. I have watched as my daughter struggled through adolescence, not fitting in, relationships, and sexual orientation. I provided a haven in the midst of traumatic circumstances and did my best to be supportive during the lows and the highs of pendulum mood swings. Throughout all this support as she dealt with personal challenges, I didn't feel that immediate affirmation and rapid medicalization were in her long-term best interest and well-being.

The gender affirming care practitioners, as well as the trans community, seemed to ignore the twenty-eight years that preceded my daughter's request for testosterone. They were not interested in the root causes of the request, and they disregarded family members' input on her background and her care. My daughters and I had been a tight and loving family unit up until transgender ideology and rapid medicalization arrived.

Parents who are transworried or transwary are not transphobic. It is time to preserve and strengthen the parent-child bond and cease demonizing and blaming parents in this debacle. Parents have the experience and ability to look further into the future than a kid immersed in an ideology. We see our kids struggling and suffering, yet parents are criticized and silenced when they express legitimate concern and doubt about the efficacy of this medicalized treatment approach.

The healthcare industry benefits from individuals electing to transition because helping people feel comfortable in their natural bodies doesn't make money. Greed has crept into the trans medicalized model. A lifelong trans patient may want more and more alterations to their bodies. The number of US clinics is growing as they grab their profits from this trend. In the past, it was rare that someone wished to engage in the medical intervention of a sex change procedure. The transition process was slow, and doctors may have been cautious. But now, some doctors are invested in medicalization because there is money to be made, and there is a push to move forward rapidly, locking in a pathway of medical dependency.

According to a report by Grand View Research, Inc., "The U.S. sex reassignment surgery market size is expected to reach USD $5 billion by 2030, growing at a CAGR of 11.25 percent from 2023 to 2030."[38]

Detransitioners, those who reverse course, often decide to return to identifying with their natal sex when they realize how deep the rabbit hole of medicalized options went. They saw the endless body and facial masculizing and feminizing cosmetic surgeries available to them in this big business. They realized that they would need one surgery after another to make themselves look like the opposite sex. This endless surgery route became less appealing, and they longed for their original, natural body and life.

Before engaging in the surgeries, most girls start by taking cross-sex hormones. I am most angry about the minimization of the adverse effects of testosterone on a woman's body and health. Because our children, teens, and young adults are being experimented on, there is not enough long-term research data on the effects of testosterone on girls' and women's bodies and health. As I began reading about the subject of gender transitioning, I started to take notes each time a detransitioner discussed the negative effects they experienced from using testosterone. I also listened to doctors and looked into medical websites for the risks of using testosterone on young women. This list is from a compilation of my notes. Of course, not all women who use the drug testosterone will have every one of these ailments. I often wonder if these risks are carefully explained to girls and women before they eagerly begin a lifelong drug dependency program. Furthermore, does their insurance policy cover these long-term ill effects from an elective and detrimental drug?

Risks and adverse effects of women taking testosterone may include:

- Hair loss, receding hairline, bald spot
- Deepening of the voice
- Acne
- Weight gain
- High blood pressure
- High cholesterol
- Increased risk of Type 2 diabetes
- Autoimmune conditions
- Metabolic syndrome and related conditions (obesity, hyperlipidemia, impaired glucose tolerance, and polycystic ovarian syndrome/PCOS)
- Erythrocytosis (which includes symptoms of blurred vision, headaches, confusion, high blood pressure, nosebleeds, itching, weakness, and tiredness)
- Cerebrovascular disease
- Hypertension
- Producing too many red blood cells (polycythemia)
- Deep vein thrombosis and/or pulmonary embolism
- Liver dysfunction
- Osteoporosis
- Pelvic pain
- Clitoral discomfort
- Atrophy in vaginal tissue
- Bladder issues
- Sleep apnea
- Increased aggression
- Irritability

- Short-term memory issues
- Loss of sexual pleasure/function
- Elimination of menstruation
- Infertility

Testosterone may initially produce what is described as a euphoric joyride, which may also suppress anxiety at first as it lifts depression. Some people who have taken it say that the artificial mood elevation sometimes doesn't last, particularly if it camouflages deep pain and underlying comorbidities. One day or year, the feeling of euphoria may crash. It may be an endless battle for these women to fight their body's natural chromosomal programming for the rest of their lives. When the initial euphoria ebbs with the transition and the honeymoon phase of changing identities is over, how will they deal with the complications of their messed-up endocrine systems, who will support them, who will profit, and who will pay for it? Compound these unanswered questions with the fact that many of these women sever their family relationships in the process of transition, and we get an even larger question: Is it all worth it?

For parents unfamiliar with surgical options that their child might be facing, let's dig in. Top surgery has two options. For female to male (FTM), a mastectomy or removal of breasts is usually the starting point surgery. For male to female (MTF), they may undergo breast augmentation, adding silicone or saline breast implants.

Bottom surgery is an endless surgery pathway for women or men wishing to change their sex identity, which may include:

- Phalloplasty to create or reconstruct a penis
- Vagina Preserving Phalloplasty to construct a new phallus while reserving the vagina

- Metoidioplasty to create a small penis from a clitoris that has become enlarged from testosterone
- Monsplasty, also known as mons pubis reduction surgery, to reshape and contour the mons pubis area
- Penile Implant, also known as a penile prosthesis, a semi-rigid rod that is surgically inserted into the phallus with testicular implants to fill out the scrotum
- Scrotal Surgery to create a realistic scrotum using the tissue from the labia majora
- Vulvoplasty to create an adult vulva
- Phallus-Preserving Vaginoplasty, also known as penile-inversion vaginoplasty, designed to create a neovagina
- Orchiectomy or castration, the removal of both testicles
- Penectomy, the removal of the penis
- Scrotectomy, the removal of the scrotum and testicles

Some individuals prefer a nonbinary look and may opt for genital nullification surgery, also called Nullo or Eunuch procedures, which involve removing all external genitalia to create a smooth transition from the abdomen to the groin. In some cases, this involves shortening the urethra. A hysterectomy is required prior to any genital nullification procedure.

Facial and cosmetic surgery options abound as well to help one resemble the opposite sex. The list goes on and on. It is a deep dive once one enters the medicalized pathway. One company's website tells its visitors, "Undergoing gender affirming surgery is a profound journey toward wholeness, authenticity and personal fulfillment." The website shows the happy faces of those who have had their surgeries and provides testimonies. Some individuals might find happiness after healing from their surgeries if they don't suffer complications. Is it not reasonable that some parents feel anger when surgeons say these surgeries will bring their children to "wholeness"?

If a full medical transition occurs for young women, it begins with testosterone, then they endure a mastectomy, and then they have another surgery for a hysterectomy. These procedures may cause them to go through menopause due to having their functional reproductive organs removed. Parents often feel angry that any doctor would consider this decision, which most consider sterilization, to be a good one for a physically healthy young woman.

No parent should have to wonder if their daughter's healthy breast tissue was thrown in a trash can, flushed down a drain, or incinerated. When someone minimizes this act of tossing out a beautiful part of their daughter's body, it feels intolerable to grieving moms and dads. It is brutal for parents to get through the day of their kid's castration or mastectomy. We are angry that such drastic, permanent, elective surgeries were sold to our kids. We are furious that there is a booming, profiting industry around these procedures.

Perhaps you understand why parents resist and are not enthusiastic about the medicalization of trans-identifying kids. Parents worldwide are losing their kids to the gender industry. Please be sensitive to parental loss and do not dismiss our grief, which is profound. It is not a trivial matter for us to lose our daughters and sons to this trans train of surgical alteration.

As already mentioned, sex reassignment surgery is a growing and profitable market. Let's not even get going on the profiteering by the pharmaceutical industry. Furthermore, when the situation crumbles, medical procedures go awry, the young person's health and finances are barely hanging on, and family relationships are left in shambles, then attorneys may reap the rewards via malpractice lawsuits from this debacle.[39]

The trans community explains that if one of their members chooses to detransition, they are experiencing an internalization of transphobia or are just in a new phase of their gender journey. Instead, those who have detransitioned say they "woke up" and could finally see the reality of their choice to embark on a pathway to permanently alter themselves. They discover that social media influences and the gender affirming care model they utilized in this process simply enabled the philosophy of "be happy in this moment" but didn't look into the future to see the long-term impact or dig into their past hurts, losses, or mental issues to see if there was a better and less-invasive path to happiness and peace with one's body.

The trans movement has a guise of love and kindness, when in reality, one can observe shaming aimed at detransitioners who return to presenting as their natal sex. It is unkind of outsiders to encourage the dissolution of the family by holding up signs and posting on social media that if the young person's family doesn't affirm their decision to change to the opposite sex, they will be their new mom. Parents are not feeling the love in this movement.

Parents are peeved with our public school and university systems that have been captured by this ideology. Other parents within a support group I belong to have younger girls on the trans train. They have expressed their distress of having schoolteachers or counselors negate the parents' input or view as soon as they hear a child say they wish to change from a girl to a boy. These educators and counselors have ascribed to an affirmation-only stance and are overstepping when they socially transition kids and use a new name and pronouns without notifying the parents.

Is it correct to demand that parents and others use pronouns that differ from the birth sex of their child? Some consider that the use of nonbinary or cross-sex pronouns may be solidifying gender confusion and a false reality. Is it possible that affirming cross-sex self-identification is actually creating suffering instead of preventing it? Without time and a doctor or therapist's differential diagnosis, it feels inappropriate and disrespectful of parents to be forced to use non-natal pronouns while the child is exploring gender or is newly influenced by transgender ideology. Social transition is not harmless; it is dangerous. No amount of wishing by our daughters that they were born as boys will change their biological reality.

Perhaps in some cases, a schoolteacher or counselor may believe there's credible evidence to only affirm when there is not. Others are so terrorized or traumatized by fear of suicide that they make decisions without including the family. But things have gotten out of hand, and some schools take their perceived authority further and call social services on parents who don't affirm trans self-identification. If schools undermine the family unit when they know nothing about the family or the kid's history, is this a correct school policy? School educators and counselors often say that they know best and children must lead. Something is terribly wrong with our school system's philosophy when parents are put down, kicked out of the driver's seat, and sometimes thrown completely out of the car of their kids' lives.

The foster care system and glitter families will be in robust need since schools deem many parents unworthy of raising their kids if they believe in biology or don't find their child wanting to change sexes to be in their long-term best interest. And in case readers and parents in the US think these issues are an American problem, the province of Ontario, Canada, is also involved in removing children from family homes and placing them in foster homes if the parents do not affirm and enable their child when they self-identify as trans. The child welfare system of Ontario has stated that they offer services to LGBT2SQ children by providing caregivers who can better meet the needs of children and youth from non-affirming families. The government website says the new foster family will provide the support the children need by "allowing them to freely and openly express their identity. This includes supporting a child or youth's choice of clothing or hairstyle, which can be important aspects of self-expression. It may also include supporting access to tools (e.g., chest binders, packers, stand-to-pee devices), gender-confirming healthcare and interventions (e.g., hormone treatments, hair removal) that for some children and youth may help them to feel their body better aligns with their gender identity."

It appears that governments in both the US and Canada are willing to overstep themselves, undermine parents, and dismantle the family unit as they collude with the trans activists' agenda.[40] Is it appropriate to champion social transition or medical intervention without consulting the parents or respecting parental views?

It seems I was lucky to have my daughter in her late twenties when she transitioned. If she had been a teen when she identified as trans, she might have been removed from my home and placed in the foster care system. How did we arrive at a place where parents who wish to "exercise caution" are labeled as abusive?

Also within parent groups are the stories of divorce occurring during the rapid transition process of a child. The court system seems more likely to award custody of the child to an affirming parent and to deny custody to a parent who questions the transition and is not in alignment with the trans train process. Our justice system seems to be joining the school system to diminish the rights of parents. Demonization of parents who are not affirming and are, instead, questioning is unacceptable. Throw in the labels of "hateful" and "transphobe," and concerned parents are often canceled by our kids, schools, and the judicial system. This attitude is profoundly troubling.

Parents are upset about social media influences and online communities on platforms such as TikTok, Instagram, Tumblr, Discord, and others. Social media sites are participating in creating a social contagion, which means the spread of ideas, behavior patterns, or attitudes through conformity or imitation.

Within the conversations in the detrans and parent communities, we have learned that there are chat rooms, trans groups, social influencers, and private social media spaces that coach kids to beat the system to get what they want, such as scripts on what to say to get their testosterone prescriptions with ease.

Reader, perhaps now is the time to browse social media with a few key search terms to see what kids are viewing. YouTube is a good place to start digging since you can find an abundance of instructional videos without barriers to view. Instagram is also a favored platform for the young trans movement. Warning: once you see these images, you cannot unsee them. You may be disturbed when you view the transition process. Please remember that each kid you see flaunting their transition has a mom and dad who are most likely devastated and grieving.

Place the following terms in your social media search:

- chest binders
- transtape
- FTM (female-to-male transition)
- MTF (male-to-female transition)
- learn how to bind and tuck
- genital affirmation surgery
- trans tutorial

The suggested search words and associated videos of these search terms are vast. In less than an hour, a curious browser can glimpse the world that parents have concerns about. Perhaps it is time to stop demonizing parents as unloving when they raise warning flags at the social influences that their beloved child is getting swept up in and sometimes swallowed by.

Who wouldn't be ticked off that gender affirming clinics happily oblige the child or young adult without fully investigating or understanding what is really going on? Have affirmation-only affiliates looked below the surface, spoken with parents, or suggested that one take time with this drastic, life-altering decision? Less than one year was the time frame from the first prescription of testosterone to a surgical mastectomy for my daughter. Who can say this rapid process will eliminate the suffering of the child if they don't care about underlying conditions or consider if the person's family is in disagreement? "Do not wait" seems to be the motto of the gender affirming practitioners.

Some young people end up getting tattoos during a youthful, whimsical moment and then are stuck with a visible reminder of that decision for the rest of their lives. Perhaps they will love that tattoo in the decades that follow, and perhaps they won't. If a young person transitions to the opposite sex during a traumatic time of confusion or clouded judgment, they are then stuck with scars and visible reminders and health issues and a slew of other adverse effects for the rest of their lives. If only a sex change were as easy to cover up, remove, or revise as a tattoo, should they later change their minds. Will the person still want to be cross-sex identified when they are forty? Sixty? Eighty?

It pushes my buttons that the requirement of therapy before cross-sex transition has become offensive to the trans community. They say only the trans-identifying kids know what they feel and what they need. Sound science that counters the kids' feelings and a lack of evidence of efficacy are overlooked or minimized. And if somehow a bit of therapy does happen, the kids are well coached on what to reveal and what to hide. They have practiced the script and so the lies go unnoticed because no one took the time to verify the history from the parents. How did parents get relegated to the lowest authority in their children's lives? How did our healthcare system evolve to this rapid push of medicalization?

I acknowledge that there are some lousy parents out there in the world. I know I'm not one of them. So, it baffles me and so many other devoted parents that we can be so unappreciated and so devalued by our kids, the school system, and gender affirming clinics. The stories vary slightly, of course, but the themes I have mentioned happen with thousands of other moms and dads. Their kids might have a different underlying condition, but the end result is the same. Little or no treatment of those conditions and the severing of ties with caring and loving parents who don't go along with this destructive pathway.

I concede that there may be gender affirming doctors who rush to medicalize because they were bamboozled by kids. Their patients had the perfect rehearsed script to check the boxes of not asking questions and proceed with great haste to a sex change procedure. As a result, they didn't think any due diligence was necessary. Their critical-thinking mind didn't care to check with a parent or dig a bit deeper into the history of the patient. Criteria was met, and they performed their prescribed "affirmation-only policy" that their clinic believes in. Perhaps they can sleep well at night … but I can't imagine how. Maybe a part of them wonders if it will work out well, but those thoughts may be quickly stifled. They have a job to do and money to make, and a full, busy schedule. Perhaps they can keep their mindset on course with the affirmative care model for a while. They can avoid reading about doctors leaving gender clinics in the UK and other parts of Europe due to their conscience. They don't listen to Jamie Reed, who blew the whistle on the gender care clinic she had previously been a part of in the US. Perhaps they are able to stuff that information away because it is too frightening to consider they might not be helping and instead are harming.

They may have started with a well-intentioned, helping heart but then got sucked into not looking at their patient in their entirety beyond their feelings of believing they were born in the wrong body. It would be disturbing to know they had been played, so they write the prescription, cut off body parts, and cross their fingers that it will work out in the end.

If reality hits a doctor and their head clears, they may have to leave their place of employment and reevaluate in their mind every patient they have ever seen and wonder if they did the right thing. That might be too hard, so they might carry on with their services for no other reason than it's hard to stop a moving train. They have staff to support them if they waver. Their enthusiasm might wane if they ever have a patient with regrets, so they say it rarely happens or don't follow up. Yet, do they ever wonder … "Is this affirmation-only track really okay?" Parents want to tell you it is not okay. Please, if you are part of the process, we parents beg you to get off the trans train and pull up the tracks. Switch to clinics that treat the whole person, explore natural alternatives for gender distress instead of drastic medicalization, and help detransitioners. Make amends.

Anger often gives way to grief and despair, or at least a movement back and forth between the emotions.

A Parent's Grief and Despair

WHEN I REALIZED in the summer of 2023 that my daughter was solidly on a rapidly moving trans train and had no interest in getting off or pausing, I spiraled. My spiral experience encompassed crying and anger cycles, and insomnia. I perseverated with hopeless thoughts, disillusionment of captured institutions, and loss of faith in the individuals within them. I felt betrayed by affirmation enthusiasts who didn't see the movement's demotion of women and the destruction of their sacred spaces as well as the dismantling of the family unit. I felt devastated as my daughter denounced her feminine beauty and her womanhood.

Everyone calls my daughters "The Girls," and to this day, people ask me, "How are the girls?" when they don't know what has happened in our family. I once adored using the phrase "the girls." I feel heartbroken that those days are over in the new world of gender identity ideology.

During periods of grief, I found myself going into dark places. On the worst of days, I felt my body's vitality draining out of me, and

I wondered if I was about to die of a broken heart. I struggled to see a reason to keep going.

I lost hope for the younger generation swept up in an ideology that denies biological reality and believes cutting off healthy breasts is to be celebrated instead of questioned. When I saw an artist create boots with a drawing glorifying a mastectomy-scarred chest with pretty rainbows around it, I felt physically sick. I lost hope in our medical system and providers who willingly engage in practices that often cause more harm than help, not only to their patients but to the families it shatters. Many kids become exhausted trying to fight nature and are distressed when they realize their health has become compromised. If those young women want their breasts back or want to try and repair the damage that the medical system enabled, they are often abandoned. If their young bodies were left alone, they might have enjoyed many years of good health.

My situation is not unique. Families all over the world are also mourning the loss of a precious daughter or son. The damage done to family relationships by transgender ideology is captured by Helena Kerschner, a detransitioner who has given many interviews about her experience and her regrets. Kerschner voiced what so many parents have told me, "There is kind of this common dynamic within the trans community. If your parents don't completely agree with you being trans and your transitioning, they are evil and horrible, and you need to cut them out of your life." I find it incomprehensible and incredibly sad that so many people on the sidelines who are not directly involved with losing a child to the trans train still find the transgender narrative appealing and blanketly endorse it.[41]

The grief a parent experiences when their kid declares they are trans is multifaceted. Most parents choose their child's name with great care, and it can be linked to another family member as well.

Trans-identifying kids usually toss out their birth names with ease and then demand the parents use a new name without any regard for the parents' feelings. Allies often add insult to injury by adopting the new name in conversation with us when they know we wish to use the birth name or also reprimanding us when we "deadname," or continue to use our beloved child's birth name that we associate with a loving bond. Not all allies reprimand, but some use the new name when we wish to use the birth name, which feels like they only respect the child's self-identification, which may be in flux, and not the parent. When further demands are made to use opposite-sex pronouns, parents are frequently demonized for resisting what feels to us like playing along with a delusion. A movement that aims to change our child's name and the way she talks, as well as all the good and love we once had, does not have our support.

Human minds have an uncanny way of perceiving biological sex, and so we feel sad when our child continues to be upset when they are misgendered. A daughter may be a biological woman living as a man. We wish the daughter could see that a girl or young woman presenting as a man is still having a female experience in not accepting or embracing her feminine features and womanhood. She may be uncomfortable with female stereotypes, but wishing she were a man is not the same as being one. We feel compelled to resist radical proclamations that she was arbitrarily assigned female at birth or that she was born in the wrong body just because she is distressed about gender or dislikes her body. We don't feel comfortable colluding in what feels like a false reality. We feel sad that she cannot see what is happening.

I feel grief and despair as I miss the days before the nightmare started. I fondly remember trips with my girls to the beach and playing in the waves together. I recall family celebrations, reunions, meals, and holidays we used to spend together. I miss hearing girl giggles in the car or in the house. I miss my daughter's natural voice. I miss her stunning, feminine beauty that she has since tried to erase. She shaved her hair short, but I can still remember combing my fingers through her long, thick hair. I miss her loving notes and cards she used to give me on special occasions. I miss being able to smile when I look at photos on the walls and on my desk and dresser, showing my daughter as an adorable kid and a beautiful young woman. Our whole family misses her. I lost a daughter, and they lost a granddaughter and a niece.

When I see my friends' daughters who are a similar age as my daughter, I am both envious and grateful that they escaped capture by the transgender ideological movement. When I see pictures of families that are still together, I want to remind them how lucky they are.

My family has always been central in my life. After losing my parents and then a daughter, my family dissolved before my eyes. On my darkest days, I found comfort in thinking that I could join my parents in the great beyond and at least have a family there where I didn't feel like I had one on earth. My purpose for the last thirty years was focused on motherhood, and after my mom's death, being a matriarch to my girls and their future families. Now, I will strive to help other moms, dads, and families in hopes that my willingness to talk about the real impact of this movement will prevent this sadness from enveloping others.

Despair can be overwhelming, and my daily focus is to survive and seek healing. Self-care to get through the day has become a part of each day's planning. Sometimes, I leave events early because I am depleted. Sometimes, I have to say no to events I want to attend because I am tired or don't want to cry to and from the events. It wears me out to put on the "everything is fine" face when I arrive and figure out how to respond each time I am asked, "How are the girls?"

When parents bump into someone who knew only of our life before our kid transitioned, and who doesn't know about our loss and our anxiety spikes, we usually just pretend things are fine until we can escape and cry more tears. We rarely ask about other people's kids in hopes they won't ask us about ours. We get good at faking normalcy and changing the subject. We spend more time alone because it is easier than acting like all is well in our lives. If we see our child's old friends from school or sports, our knees go weak when we see their unaltered bodies, and we may get woozy if we see family photos celebrating a wedding, a new baby, a family vacation, or a holiday. So many triggers can amplify our pain.

The façade that we are well is exhausting. The trauma and tears from it all can go on for years. Hope for our children and families is fleeting and often nonexistent. We soak in any kindness that might come our way. A thoughtful word or gesture can help us get through the day. We try not to become bitter that an ideological movement swept up our kids and stole them from our homes and lives. We stifle our anger that others enable, champion, and celebrate that process. When parents are betrayed and forgotten, we mourn in the privacy of our homes. The solitude of our loss envelops us. Our tears are rarely witnessed by others. I am one of those parents, and we need to rethink a medical and educational model that devastates the family in such a profound way.

Lynn Chadwick, a parent in a support group in which I belong, described her sadness. "The grief we carry is so very heavy and difficult to heal from because there is no resolution. It took me five years to find enough peace to feel like I was alive again. So many tears but even more emptiness. I was going through the bare minimum motions. I think it needed to take that long. And it's still hard. But I was eventually able to release my children. They will make their own decisions, and I have no control over that."

Yes, I got therapy and attended support groups, researched, read books, and tried to focus on what was still good in my life. However, I am a mom who doesn't have blinders on. I don't think transgender medicalization is a good choice for my daughter or for most young people.

I join thousands of parents globally in advocating for our daughters to accept their natural bodies and for the cessation of the harmful notion that only a "new one" will bring happiness. "Trans joy" or "gender euphoria" seems to be the motto of transgender youth today. Parents feel grief knowing that these joy and euphoria periods are likely fleeting highs, and we are locked out of the conversation to warn our children.

I can imagine being enchanted by the idea of shedding one's current self and becoming someone different. I remember graduating from high school and going to a college in another state. I realized that no one knew me at my new school, and all the labels or perceptions of me were unknown. I felt exhilarated by creating a new self, being someone different. I envisioned how I wanted to be seen, made decisions on how to present myself that way, and began acting the part until it felt more natural. In my case, I had been labeled as shy and awkward in high school, definitely not in the popular crowd, and I wanted to be more socially at ease and more graceful in my interactions. I indeed blossomed into someone quite different from my teenage self. I liked the new me, and it stuck. Some people who meet me today do not suspect how introverted and socially inept I used to be. Today's trans model takes this desire to create a new persona too far. It may be acceptable to try different ways of presenting oneself, but the trans narrative suggests irreversibly harming the physical body, which crosses the line. Add in the shattering of the family unit, and this medicalization pathway is the most destructive ideology I have witnessed in my family.

Some kids transition to be trendy or rebellious; however, many moms know their daughters have tremendous pain. We saw it firsthand. We know it is still there, deep down. We can see that she found a solution to her unbearable anguish by changing her name and pronouns, covering her body with tattoos, donning a new wardrobe, cutting her long hair shorter and shorter, taking testosterone, bulking up, growing facial hair, and finally, having her breasts removed with a mastectomy. We can understand that this process may be her trying to erase herself while still living as the only option she saw in her attempt to survive what must be unbearable pain. We can see the appeal of a quick fix and chasing euphoria instead of exploring options to heal trauma or loss or considering the complexity of her feelings, which might take many years. We suspect our daughter thought we represented her old life, so we needed to be cut out of her new life so we would not attempt to persuade her to pause or remain a woman, which would just remind her of the past she had tried to erase and leave behind. Moms are often a casualty of their daughter's new identity. Just because we can see a possible reason why we are dropped from our daughters' lives does not mean it is reasonable for us to be happy about it or celebrate this tremendous loss.

Observations and conversations with other parents have indicated that these experiences are not unique. Parents are getting the impression that some of the younger generation have lost the sense of value for family and elder wisdom. Instead, the thought seems to be that traditional family units are disposable, renamed as bio-families, and that parents and elders are relics of past ideologies that no longer pertain to living in the modern world of today. This youthful philosophy saddens us profoundly.

Most parents, including me, have deep compassion for those struggling with mental distress and confusion. It takes courage to ask for help and time to explore treatment options. We support our daughters in measures they might undertake to heal their trauma and pain. But sometimes, trans-identifying kids displace their unhealed pain, targeting their parents. It can be crushing for parents to see an ideology suggest that healthy breasts and functioning, healthy reproductive organs and genitalia must be sacrificed to become authentically whole. Anguished parents who watch their kids demand attention and celebration while they are left to mourn in solitude cannot believe what has happened in our culture and to our beloved children who got swallowed up by transgender ideology.

In the darkest hours of my life, during my sixtieth year, I began to share with close friends and some family. I received mixed responses. I was grateful for those willing to compassionately listen, which helped me heal. On the other hand, my experience was often minimized. At times, comments from others made me feel like I was being scoffed at and dismissed because I couldn't possibly add value to the conversation. I was lumped in with all those uninformed, uneducated, and old-fashioned parents who couldn't add perspective to a transgender narrative that had to be guarded at all costs.

A few dear friends witnessed my pain and supported me when I cried and spiraled. Others were super busy and just didn't have time to spend with me on it. I get that; I really do. Not only do others have a multitude of responsibilities to juggle, but they also have their own problems to carry. I appreciated the time I was given so at least I didn't have to lie that things were going well. This topic is new to some people, and it can be overwhelming to understand. In some cases, it was just too much to handle when they had their own worries. I have no hard feelings. We all do the best we can with the knowledge, experience, skills, and time that we have now.

Parents have expressed within support groups that every relationship they have changes when their kid becomes involved in the gender ideological movement. A few relationships become stronger. Many diminish, fracture, or dissolve. We avoid some people just so we don't have to talk about it. Others avoid us, saying that they hope we feel better soon and that we learn how to affirm.

When one loses a kid to other causes, such as an accident, suicide, or cancer, the parents may receive an outpouring of condolences. When one loses a child to the trans train, the parents are alone. There are no funerals or celebration of life events for our losses. Birthdays and holidays are dreaded and bring our loss into acute focus. Parents mourn privately, often crying themselves to sleep or crying as they wake when they realize the nightmare is real. Very few people will acknowledge this kind of loss. And if they are in the affirmation camp where they were told that whatever the child wants, parents must accept, then they may tell parents to work harder at acceptance.

I heard comments such as, "If they are happy now, that is the only thing that matters." My problem with that comment is that they may not be truly happy because the underlying issues might not have been treated properly, if at all. And the carnage in the family is completely overlooked. Whenever I see a kid who identifies as trans, I want to say, "How is your mom?" Because behind that kid is often a mom or other family member with a broken heart. Even the families I know that decided to affirm their child's transition still mourn privately. Bereft mothers and fathers and other family members are often ignored other than receiving a few platitudes, a pat on the back of the hand, and suggestions to get more therapy and get over it and accept it. Some parents have even been called "bad parents" because of what happened to their children.

Parents can go through the motions of the day. We can compartmentalize to a point and pretend to be doing well in public. Privately, our days, and particularly our nights, are a nightmare that we cannot wake up from. We often have insomnia that makes nights a living hell. Nothing gives us peace of mind because the core issue remains unresolved, and the tragedy continues. Some things we used to think were important often seem trivial and no longer relevant to us. Everything we see looks different through the lens of losing a daughter or son.

Beyond the circle of our families, parents also feel sadness in a larger context. Our hopes to raise our daughters to become the next generation of women leaders to help us all navigate the challenges of living in today's modern age have been dashed. Collectively, our girls may have had the opportunity to powerfully break female stereotypes and glass ceilings that held them back and to show other young girls that they could be strong and amazing women today. Instead, our daughters chose to present as nonbinary or as men now. We feel abandoned and betrayed. It is an excruciating feeling when we see our daughters publicly show that they wish to be nothing like their mothers.

I love photography and was one of those moms who took lots of pictures of my girls growing up. I loved to take pictures at their birthday parties, our holiday celebrations, vacations, and just goofing off. I have all those photos carefully curated in albums that are too painful to view now. I suspect if my youngest daughter saw them today, she would throw them away since they represent an old life in her perceived wrong body that holds no value to the new persona she has created. I will continue to preserve those memories and milestones, even though it all seems so futile at times.

Today, I move about the world with a cloud hanging over me. I miss the special bond I had as a trio of "mom and her girls." I long for the ability of the three of us to gather with extended family, which no longer occurs. My grief sometimes transmutes into a hardened numbness, and laughter and joy can be elusive. Sometimes, I pretend well enough that people don't see my devastation and loss. Who wants to be around a "walking wounded" mom? This façade is heavy, and sometimes I just stay home alone so I don't have to fake being okay all the time. Sadly, my story is not unique. My research revealed that thousands of other parents are in profound sadness and grief too. How did our greatest joy in life turn into our deepest agony?

A poem titled "You Don't Just Lose Someone Once" by Donna Ashworth resonates with me regarding the loss of my daughter. Losing someone is not a one-time loss; we lose them again and again every day. You can find the poem by searching online.

It can be difficult for parents to find meaning in their lives once tragedy and loss have gone deep and wide. Finding peace and healing can take years. We will never be the same. We will redefine ourselves, but it is a process that takes time. There are no adequate words to describe the suffering this movement perpetrates; however, I have done my best to shed light on the parental despair I have felt and the sorrow other parents have shared with me. I acknowledge and hold within this chapter the collective grief and pain of parents who have experienced the loss of a child in this manner.

Thankfully, my grief can flow into gratitude for those who have stopped participating in a medicalization model for trans-identified youth and are standing up to this harmful ideology.

A Parent's Gratitude

I AM GRATEFUL THAT BRAVE PEOPLE are speaking out with their concerns about the gender industry. Thankfully, many people are now willing to look at the deep-seated issues that lie within a person who identifies as trans. Many critical thinkers are beginning to see through the motivations of those pushing for and rushing medicalization and are shifting to protecting the well-being of vulnerable children and youth. I have seen pictures of protesters opposing medicalization procedures for young people, holding placards saying things like:

Self-love not surgery
Don't trans the gay away
Gender nonconforming teens need love not mastectomies

I am grateful to be seeing hints that members of all political parties are concerned. There is a new term for the moment someone realizes that something isn't right with gender ideology, and it is called "Peak Trans."[42] Once you see the harm befalling children and women, you can't unsee it. Perhaps this book and the resources therein have shifted your paradigm. If so, it is time to do something about it.

Many liberal parents are becoming disillusioned with their party and its lack of understanding of what is really happening to kids and the harm befalling them to an affirmation-only model and robust medicalization push. "I've been a Democrat my whole life until this whole trans thing hit home," said an anonymous parent in the support group I engage in. The idea that the trans movement is progressive, happy, and loving dissipates quickly when a left-leaning parent loses a child to it.

Because some Democrats demonize those on the political right who advocate for the cessation of cross-sex medicalization of minors, it might be surprising that many on the political left also oppose hormonal and surgical medicalization of minors. Kara Dansky, author of *The Reckoning*, says, "Some of the fiercest opposition to 'gender identity' all over the world comes from people who consider themselves as being (or having been) on the political left. The reason that most people don't know this is that our party leaders and the media consistently ignore us and actively suppress our views." I hope more liberals will become vocal and advocate for change. I also hope both US political parties can come together to address the harms of medicalizing our children in this manner.

Earlier in this book, I mentioned courageous spokespeople who are waving the red flag in this reckless "affirmation-only" care model of our youth. I would like to acknowledge and express gratitude for a few additional people who have decided to speak out against this fast-tracked pathway.

Jamie Reed

In *The Free Press* on February 9, 2023, Jamie Reed wrote an article entitled "I Thought I Was Saving Trans Kids. Now I'm Blowing the

Whistle." Reed wrote, "There are more than 100 pediatric gender clinics across the US. I worked at one. What's happening to children is morally and medically appalling."[43,44]

Reed describes herself as a forty-two-year-old St. Louis native, a queer woman, and politically to the left of Bernie Sanders. She also says she is married to a trans man (biological woman). She worked as a case manager at a clinic, which was heavily into providing hormone prescriptions. The majority of the young people who came to that clinic received hormone prescriptions. Reed left the clinic in 2022 because she could no longer participate in what was happening there. She states, "By the time I departed, I was certain that the way the American medical system is treating these patients is the opposite of the promise we make to 'do no harm.' Instead, we are permanently harming vulnerable patients in our care."

Reed continues, "To begin transitioning, the girls needed a letter of support from a therapist—usually one we recommended—who they had to see only once or twice for the green light. To make it more efficient for the therapists, we offered them a template for how to write a letter in support of transition. The next stop was a single visit to the endocrinologist for a testosterone prescription. That's all it took."

Reed describes girls coming to the clinic with many comorbidities, such as depression, anxiety, ADHD, eating disorders, and autism. This statement confirms what parents say within the support groups I belong to. She also reports that the doctors privately recognized that this trend might be part of a social contagion, which is also widely spoken about in the news, publications, and interviews.

Reed felt that these young people understood little of the profound impacts of medicalization. The center she worked for downplayed the negative consequences of the change in their bodies and minds. Testosterone, which is used to trick the body into thinking it is the opposite sex, may cause lifelong medical treatment with medication to control blood pressure and cholesterol, sleep apnea, diabetes, and other medical challenges.

She mentioned that she found it disturbing that the center lacked regard for the rights of parents. The doctors "saw themselves as more informed decision-makers over the fate of these children." In her affidavit to Missouri's attorney general, Reed shared,

"Parents would come into the Center wanting to discuss research and ask questions. The clinicians would dismiss the research that the parents had found and speak down to the parents. When parents suggested that they wanted only therapy treatment, not cross-sex hormones or puberty blockers, doctors treated those parents as if the parents were abusive, uneducated, and willing to harm their own children."

This culture of negating parents' concerns, described by Reed, is what I experienced, what parents in my support groups have experienced, and it confirms what I've found in my research. This dismissal of parents is not acceptable. I recommend reading the complete affidavit of Jamie Reed.[45]

Erin Friday

Friday is a California attorney, a mom, and a leader within the parent advocacy group Our Duty. She has appeared in numerous publications and interviews, including a YouTube video entitled, "Mom Explains What It Took to Rescue Daughter From Transgenderism." She comes from the political left and is a hard-working advocate for legislation changes to stop harming our children and young adults.[46]

Hannah Barnes

Barnes, an investigations producer at BBC Newsnight, authored the book, *Time to Think: The Inside Story of the Collapse of the Tavistock's*

Gender Service for Children. The UK is waking up to this harmful pathway. In March 2022, an independent report commissioned by Britain's National Health Service found that the type of care provided at Tavistock was "not safe or viable as a long-term option for the care of young people with gender-related distress."[47]

Marcus Evans

Evans wrote an article for *Quillette* on January 17, 2020, titled "Why I Resigned from Tavistock: Trans-Identified Children Need Therapy, Not Just 'Affirmation' and Drugs."

The article says, "When doctors always give patients what they want (or think they want), the fallout can be disastrous, as we have seen with the opioid crisis." At least thirty-five psychologists have also left the clinic, he says.[48]

Helen Joyce

Joyce is a journalist and former staff writer for *The Economist*. She wrote the book *Trans: When Ideology Meets Reality* in 2021. Her book took a deep dive of inquiry into gender identity ideology, which focuses on self-declared gender identity over biology. She now works at a startup human rights organization, Sex Matters, which campaigns for clarity about the two sexes, male and female, in law and in life.

Abigail Shrier

Shrier is a writer for *The Wall Street Journal*. As a journalist, she dug deep into the trans epidemic. Her book *Irreversible Damage: The Transgender Craze Seducing Our Daughters* is based on her investigation after talking to agonized parents, girls, and detransitioners who bitterly regret what they did to themselves. She also discusses counselors and doctors who enable gender transitions.

Amber Alt, PhD

Alt shares her educated perspective in her 2023 book, *It's Not Transphobic to Say Your Daughter Is a Girl: The Wise Lesbian Guide for Progressives*. She presents the long-term risk of medicalization of young girls and women through the lens of sociology and gay and lesbian history. Important historical context is explained in a rational manner. Transgender ideology may be the latest iteration of gay conversion therapy.

Kara Dansky

Currently in the US, Democrats have fallen behind Republicans in efforts to protect our children and women's rights, but the tide is turning. For those who do not understand what has happened politically in America, read Kara Dansky's book, *The Reckoning: How the Democrats and the Left Betrayed Women and Girls*. Dansky describes herself as a radical feminist and lifelong Democrat. In her book, she exposes the invasion by men into female-only spaces, the harming of children, and the silencing, punishment, cancellation, and even violence against women who speak out. Both parties need to come together to stop the harm to children and young adults.

Miriam Grossman, MD

Dr. Grossman wrote a book in 2023 entitled *Lost in Trans Nation: A Child Psychiatrist's Guide Out of the Madness*. Dr. Grossman offers no-nonsense research and wisdom for parents and others concerned with this disturbing trend. If you forgot your science and biology education, she will remind you of it. She also shows how the affirmation model is a dangerous idea that is infecting our schools and the medical system. Homes and families are being torn apart, and Dr. Grossman will fortify you as to what you can do about it. Education is the first step, and that can be achieved by reading this science-based book. The appendix has suggestions on how to deal with schools and Child Protective Services, and she also shows you how to find a therapist and employ internet accountability tools. Her book is packed with power.

James Esses

Esses believes that gender identity ideology undermines free speech, destroys careers, and tears families apart. In his writings, he discusses identity politics, where one's "lived experience" is prized above all else and where groups of individuals are placed into categories of "privilege" or "victimhood." "This mass delusion, that biological sex is a matter of choice, poses a danger to young people on an unprecedented scale. In nursery schools, under-fives are made to listen to stories about transgender toddlers, read to them by men in sexualized drag costumes. Confused teenagers and their parents are being taught that it is possible to be born in the wrong body and are encouraged to believe that the best response to disliking their body is to have irreversible chemical and surgical treatment."

Esses is fighting back against the ideological capture of society. This ideology is not progressive but rather regressive. Victim hierarchies being taught in schools with "Wheel of Privilege" charts split people into "power" or "marginalized" sections. He is concerned that this narrative might promote a feeling that it pays to be seen as a victim instead of instilling a sense of resiliency.[49]

Leor Sapir

Leor Sapir discusses the institutional capture of education and medicine by gender ideology.[50] Sapir is a fellow at the Manhattan Institute (MI). In his work at the MI, Dr. Sapir applies his research and academic experience to policy matters, concentrating on issues of gender identity and transgenderism. His inaugural essay in *City Journal* (Winter 2022) explores a series of recent court rulings on transgenderism, demonstrating how bad ideas translate from fringe academic theory into law and policy. Previous pieces for *City Journal* explored evolving athletic guidelines and media coverage surrounding transgender issues.

Dr. Stephen Levine

Dr. Stephen Levine is a clinical professor of psychiatry and author of five books on sex and love. He has been the senior editor of three editions of the *Handbook of Clinical Sexuality for Mental Health Professionals*. In the last several years, most of his academic output has involved trans matters. Informed consent, evidence evaluation, ethics, and the description of a life cycle perspective are topics that he is often called upon to discuss. These topics converge into an interest in a psychotherapy-first approach to concerned individuals and their parents. During a presentation by Dr. Levine, I heard him say that parents are transworried or transwary, not transphobic, which I borrowed for this book. Thank you, Dr. Levine, for understanding parents!

Colin Wright

Dr. Colin Wright is an evolutionary biology PhD, Manhattan Institute Fellow and Academic Advisor for the Society for Evidence-Based Gender Medicine. When Dr. Wright was asked if sex categories of male and female are real, immutable, and binary or merely social constructs, Wright's answer was, "Real (that's just the way it is and we all know it), immutable (it can't be changed), and binary (there are only two sexes, not three or four or fifty-seven). He goes on to say, "Gender ideology seeks to portray sex as so incomprehensibly complex and multivariable that our traditional practice of classifying people as either male or female is grossly outdated and should be abandoned for a revolutionary concept of 'gender identity.' This new system holds that males shouldn't be barred from female sports, women's prisons, or any other space previously segregated as long as they 'identify' as female."[51]

Riley Gaines

Riley Gaines, also known as Riley Gaines Barker, is an American former competitive swimmer from Gallatin, Tennessee, who competed for the University of Kentucky NCAA swim team. She was the 2022 Southeastern Conference Women's Swimming and Diving Scholar-Athlete of the Year. Gaines is fighting to save women's sports; their hard-earned achievements are being stolen by biological men. She also addresses that women's and girls' most vulnerable spaces—shelters, locker rooms, and restrooms—are no longer safe. She speaks across the country and has created the Riley Gaines Center to build a movement to stand up for women's sports and common-sense American values.[52]

Martina Navratilova

Navratilova is a Czech-American former professional tennis player who won fifty-nine major titles: eighteen singles titles, thirty-one women's doubles, and ten mixed doubles finals. She does not believe that biological men, now calling themselves trans women, should be playing against biological female players. The USTA (United States Tennis Association) seems to have succumbed to trans-activist pressure if they allow biological males to play in the professional women's draw in tournaments. Navratilova is standing up in support of women's sports despite the onslaught of bullying and cruel defamation she has received.

Trans women (biological men) who try to dethrone women athletes, some of whom trained their whole lives for their chance to shine in competition only to be taken off the podium by a man who would like to be a woman, is not okay with me and many others. In addition to Gaines and Navratilova speaking up, some transsexuals are also contributing opinions.

Corinna Cohn

Cohn is a writer, podcaster, and activist from Indiana. Cohn, a biological male who identifies as transsexual, states, "It is absurd and unreal that liberal organizations are turning their backs on women's rights." Cohn was diagnosed with gender identity disorder at age fifteen and underwent surgical transition at age nineteen. In 2019, Cohn became involved with patient advocacy, and in 2022 began organizing to support legislation that regulates the gender medicalization of minors. Corinna has met with legislators and given testimony in Indiana, Texas, and Ohio.[53]

J.K. Rowling

On the podcast "The Witch Trials of J.K. Rowling, Chapter 5: The Tweets," Rowling expressed, "Time will tell whether I've got this wrong. I can only say that I've thought about it deeply and hard and long. I've listened, I promise, to the other side, and I believe there is something dangerous about this movement, and it must be challenged."

Scrolling through articles about the author's tweets, I saw a picture of a trans activist holding up a sign at a rally that said, "Rot in Hell Rowling." These harsh words are another example of the poor ambassadorship of transgender activism.

Despite the flak that the author of *Harry Potter* is getting from the trans community, I am heartened that she tweeted on May 13, 2022, a shoutout: "Allison Bailey, Keira Bell and Sonia Appleby. One day, books will be written looking back at the full impact gender identity ideology had on vulnerable youth, women's rights and freedom of speech here in the UK, and these women will rightly be seen as heroines."[54]

The TERF Movement

TERF, Trans-Exclusionary-Radical Feminist, once a derogatory term, has been reclaimed as a badge of honor by many women fighting to protect women's sex-based rights and the protection of children and vulnerable LGB people. TERFs know that "gender identity" obscures the reality of sex, and they are committed to protecting and advancing the interests of women and girls as a sex class. Thank you to all the TERFs out there, working tirelessly on behalf of women and girls!

The scope of this book does not allow me to highlight all those who are standing up to oppose a drastic medicalized pipeline for our kids. Hope is on the horizon because many different groups are now speaking out from all sectors of society: liberals and conservatives, LGB groups and transsexual people, detransitioners, parents, and clinic workers. Why? Because they have come to believe that more harm than help is now occurring. Since so many people are seeing the negative impact of transgender ideology and are bravely speaking up about it, there is hope it might begin to subside. Any ideology that advocates the dissolution of the family, hooks young people into medical dependency, makes a profit from them, and denigrates women should be highly suspect.

I am grateful for those who came before me to help me learn and grow in my understanding of this complex topic. Let's keep the discussion open.

The Gender Party

THIS PIECE, WRITTEN BY JENNIFER WESSON, appeared in PITT Substack (Parents of Inconvenient Truths and Trans) on July 24, 2023. Both the author and PITT gave permission to reprint the essay in this book. When I read *The Gender Party*, it reflected my experience, and I did not want to paraphrase the presentation. Those who have read the book *1984* by George Orwell will recognize the parallels to that book. Wesson begins her thoughts with a quote from the book.

> *"The party told you to reject the evidence of your eyes and ears. It was their final, most essential command."*
> — George Orwell in *1984*

So, you aren't a member of the gender party. At least you don't think you are. You haven't really considered it. You've had no time. Your days were spent working and raising your family. You weren't even sure it was a real party and it had never meant anything to you any way. After all, you consider yourself liberal, at the very least moderate, and don't want to harm the most vulnerable members of society. If you have ever thought about gender ideology, you might have said, "What's the big deal? It isn't harming anyone. Adults should be free to live as they please." You're a big tent person and proud of it.

Then the most shocking, unbelievable thing happens. Out of the blue, your child announces that they aren't their biological sex any longer. They are now magically, 100% the other sex. And they assure you that there is nothing, absolutely nothing, you will ever be able to do to change their mind. And should you try, your child will remove you from their life.

This is when you discover, although you aren't a member, the gender party has a hold on many facets of your life—schools, the medical profession, the mental health community, the mainstream media. Worse yet, if you do not pledge fealty, you may lose your child, your job and your friends and family. Welcome to the party.

You will soon discover that the gender party regards your child, whatever their age, as a fully formed adult who knows what they want for themselves and will never waiver in this belief. This wouldn't be so bad if it was just an idea, a belief with no consequences. But the gender party demands that your children be medicalized and then perhaps, move on to surgery. Sometimes immediately. Not after a year of waiting or months of therapy, but right now—the minute your child has decided they are "trapped in the wrong body." The only real thing now is their belief.

The gender party controls everyone and everything. They don't need to provide any evidence that what they do is good. There is no debate. It is a fact because the party deems it so. Everyone must believe this. The gender party is a force for good, lifesaving even. And woe to those who ask for a shred of evidence or express a hint of doubt. The gender party will try to ruin you and take away the one thing you are trying to protect, your child.

Now that your child is in the gender party—a fresh, wide-eyed recruit—you learn that the people who you thought knew you and your child best are card carrying, dues paying members of the gender party. They don't understand your doubts. Because if your child says they are another sex—they are! That's how this works.

You will learn that those who succeed in escaping the gender party need to act early and sometimes take radical action. But, sigh, you have other children and a job and so many things that make it impossible to change your entire life and move some place (where?!) that the gender party hasn't taken hold. If your child is already of legal age, you have almost no leverage. And you realize that if you dare to question your adult child's new identity (an identity that may have been formed in just a few months by googling their questions and talking to strangers online), you may be cut off. The gender party tells all its members that anyone who doesn't believe absolutely in the gender religion must be exiled and cut out of your child's life. This seems cultish to you, but you say nothing to avoid charges of heresy.

People you thought would have your back—maybe your mother or your brother, that amazing coworker, your best friend—are now questioning you. They talk to each other and agree that your child must be affirmed. And that surely you will come to see the gender party knows best. You can understand that some of them are fearful of retaliation by the gender party. They cannot take the chance and stand by your side, but you remain horrified by the betrayal. You have nowhere to turn with your anger and fear. You are alone.

And then a "helpful" person sends a text or email accusing you of being a bigot, a TERF, a transphobe, a bad parent. Or, the ultimate insult, they imply that you would rather have a dead kid than a trans kid. In their eyes, you are a monster. There is no chance to explain that your child might be gay or on the autism spectrum or suffer from severe anxiety or trauma. None of which have anything to do with becoming the other sex. None of these matters. The gender party has the answer for every mental anguish and social problem that ever existed. Not just *the* answer but the *only* answer.

You thought you knew your kid. You were there for everything, every tear, every problem over the years. But apparently, you knew nothing. Their special inner feeling, their new identity, which they confirm by searching the internet and is further affirmed in chat rooms and video games, is now all that matters. Teachers who know them for one semester or a few months of school, along with thirty other kids, know your child best. They withhold your child's new name and identity because your child must be protected from you at all costs. You have changed from being the one person who put your child's welfare and happiness above all else to becoming your child's greatest enemy.

The doctors and therapists, you soon learn, are the most fervent believers in the gender party. They have no questions for you, or your child, save one—how do you identify? However your child responds at this moment is the only truth, no matter the consequences of the medical treatments which they happily prescribe on the first visit. Your kid will give "informed consent," a kid that doesn't ever think of themselves at age 30 or 40 and what it might be to live for decades pretending to be the opposite sex. And, of course, they are not considering that they may want children someday. Children aren't thinking of having children. But the gender party can make sure they never do.

But what about biology you ask. Must we relearn everything you were ever taught about biology and history? Clownfish are the answer. Intersex people are cited to prove that you can change sex. But you know that your child isn't a clownfish and is not intersex.

You learn that your child was "assigned" a sex at birth. The nurses and doctors just decided for reasons unknown and possibly nefarious, what gender your child was. The DNA tests and ultrasounds are wrong as well, as science no longer exists. You learn there are forty-seven genders and that genders can change all the time. Sex is dead. It has no meaning and is just used as an excuse to discriminate against trans people and all the other-gendered people.

You soon discover that yes, even the Holocaust was the source of suffering for no, not the Jewish people, but primarily transgender people. And of course, you are probably a Nazi yourself if you think differently.

Historical figures, mostly women, it seems, are also now being reclaimed with their rightful trans identity. Joan of Arc and Louisa May Alcott were not feminist heroes but trans men.

Trans women are literally women, you learn. That's it. A fact. Women now have penises. Women are now committing rape and murder at higher rates than ever recorded throughout history.

Trans women are also miraculously better at sports than natal women for reasons no one can discern. When competing against women, now known as uterus havers, trans women win all the competitions and titles. Any "cis" women objecting to this are just sore losers. "Cis" is the new label you must go by if you don't despise the body you were born with and want to alter it. You are told this is a great privilege to be "cis" and that trans women suffer much more than any cis woman ever could or ever will, no matter what has happened to you as a "cis" woman.

You go underground. You join groups that vet members. Here you can speak freely because all members know what you are going through and share your horror of the gender party.

You are looking for evidence to stop the gender party from destroying your precious child. But the gender party won't consider anything that might contradict its dogmas. Remember the party slogan—"no debate." The gender party has your child, and seemingly, all of society in its grip. You hang on, hoping someday to save your child and end the gender party forever.

An Open Letter to Teens and Young Adults

TO THE YOUNG PERSON who is thinking about transitioning or has already begun the process, please consider that medicalization may not be the solution to your pain or fulfill your desire for happiness. The search for happiness can be elusive and fleeting. It may be appealing to grab onto a quick-fix idea, but be skeptical of promises by strangers, particularly when those promises involve drugs. Be cautious of social influencers because they may mislead you. Explore options and the possibility of being happy without altering your body. People who encourage you to subvert your relationship with your parents may be manipulating you for their purposes. Consider the benefits that might come from investing in deep and meaningful family relationships in which your care has been their dedicated focus.

It takes time to explore your feelings and hone your critical thinking skills. The influencers who try to persuade you (or perhaps already have) to use chemicals and alter your body surgically may not know your nuanced past and may not actually have your best interests in their motives. Some people will deliberately misguide you for money (such as activists, clinics, gender providers, and the pharmaceutical industry) or fame (such as gender-related social media influencers who want more followers and likes). Some people may have been captured by ideological theory or not understand a history of homosexual mistreatment and suppression. Others do not have a solid base of biological and scientific education. Some are relying on flawed research instead of evidence-based studies. Be careful before you choose irreversible and permanent changes to your body and your health based on feelings because feelings change over time. You may be able to change features to resemble the opposite sex at this stage of your life, but you cannot actually become the opposite sex, and you may not actually want to appear like the opposite sex for decades to come.

There are times when a pharmaceutical intervention is the right choice to stabilize one's mood or to treat a mental issue or illness after a diagnostic evaluation is performed by a board-certified psychiatrist. Other doctors and professionals may need to assist in sorting out your distress or confusion and then show you several options that might help you. Do not make drastic decisions that have long-term consequences from a self-diagnosis as a result of watching social media videos, taking an online questionnaire, or talking with friends. Those are not accurate and well-rounded resources for your research. They do not have your best interests in mind. You and your body are too valuable to let strangers and new ideological movements influence you without careful analysis and thoughtful long-term considerations.

Place your family first, as they know you best. Work to deepen and strengthen family relationships because you will need them as you grow older and experience challenges and difficulties in your life. Tap into elder wisdom and experience. Of course, some parents are truly abusive. Develop true discernment between genuine abuse and the deep, loving concern that a devoted parent shows you. Do not rush a monumental decision that will affect and alter the rest of your life and your health.

Please spend more time outside in nature and moving your body through sports or exercise than you spend on your electronic devices. Read books instead of tapping into social media. Soak in the beauty of the earth. Travel the world and learn about history and other cultures and belief systems. Practice self and body acceptance rather than succumbing to the notion that the natural body needs alteration. Be kind to all beings, especially to yourself.

Conclusion and Possible Solutions

IT IS TIME TO WRAP UP and provide ideas and possible solutions to change the trajectory of losing our young girls and boys to irreversible damage to their bodies and to their long-term health and well-being.

Problem: The tendency to ignore or downplay detransitioners.

Many of my views have been shaped by detransitioners, who have the inside scoop of this movement. They have a unique view of life before they entered the transgender world, what happened to them within that sphere, and why they left it. Some individuals who medicalized seem to have created a happy life for themselves; however, the distorted view that most people who have transitioned are doing well does not address the ever-growing numbers of individuals who found they had made a mistake. As mentioned earlier, Reddit's detransition group had over fifty thousand members at the time of this book's publication, and the number is growing.[55]

To ignore or downplay detransitioners and their complications and regrets is a disservice to anyone who is attempting to undo physical and health-related damage, as well as to improve mental health and repair relationships that suffered or were severed during the medicalization time of their lives.

> **Solution:** Media and social outlets can interview detransitioners to learn from them. Members of the medical community can take care of these wounded individuals and do everything they can to help them heal from the trauma they experienced.

Problem: Young people are medicalized too quickly.

Children may not be capable of giving informed consent for drastic interventions, which will affect their health for the rest of their lives. The agenda to medicalize young people as quickly as possible without addressing underlying trauma or mental issues and commonalities is not a responsible path. Be careful about relying on feelings and flawed research to support rapid transition procedures. Locking in a *feeling* with drastic medicalization seems like a bad idea, as many detransitioners have discovered.

> **Solution:** Check out SEGM, the Society for Evidence-Based Gender Medicine. This international group of over a hundred clinicians and researchers is concerned about the lack of quality evidence for the use of hormonal and surgical interventions as first-line treatment for young people with gender dysphoria. They provide studies and spotlight the latest news on gender medicine topics.[56]

Consider the cessation of cross-sex hormone prescriptions unless the individual has undergone a waiting period of several years with a documented, extensive exploration of every facet of their reasons for desiring transition, their personality beyond gender, and underlying conditions. If girls request a mastectomy or boys wish to remove their genitals, they must be twenty-five years old and then wait two years after their initial surgical consultation. During their waiting period, they must also provide proof of exploring other options, which might include therapy that addresses all underlying conditions. This process will decrease possible negligence lawsuits against surgeons.

Problem: Some people identify as trans to avoid the homosexual stigma.

There will also always be homosexual people, those who have same-sex desires, in the world. In some countries, homosexuality is punishable by death, and in that circumstance, a sex change procedure may save their life. In most countries, that extreme law is not present, and therefore, caution should be exercised before chemical and surgical alteration is encouraged. In America and Europe, there has been a historical context of mistreatment of gay people. Conversion therapy practices are inappropriate approaches to same-sex attraction.

Solution: Teach the history of homosexual oppression. Let's stop "transing the gay away," our modern-day agenda aimed at eradicating homosexual expression.

Problem: Kids are encouraged to medicalize when they even question or experiment with atypical gender interests.

Kids and young adults do not always look like or desire activities and interests of typical gender stereotypes of masculine and feminine.

> **Solution:** Allow young people to be different. Let girls be tomboys, and allow boys to express feminine characteristics without shaming them for it. Stop pushing young, non-conforming people to undergo chemical or surgical medical intervention.

Problem: Images and social media platforms glorify self-harming behavior and invasive procedures.

Enabling and celebrating maladaptive coping mechanisms is not an appropriate response to self-harming behaviors. Let's not consider it cool to undergo or flaunt radical, irreversible surgical procedures.

> **Solution:** Do not showcase and promote photography/videos, art, and fashion that glorifies self-harming behavior, such as depicting a scarred mastectomy chest surrounded by colorful rainbows. Replace trans art or photography with an emphasis that depicts the beauty of natural bodies, particularly feminine bodies.

Problem: Influencers use social media to attract vulnerable youth who are in distress, encouraging them to question their biological or natal sex and take drastic action.

There is a lapse in critical thinking for enabling kids' feelings gleaned from watching YouTube, TikTok, Instagram, Snapchat, and videos from other social media platforms. When one sees a social media post saying, "My friends on the internet are essentially raising me as trans," it is confirmation that social media influencers are indoctrinating kids into the world of "transgender" ideology. Social media is not a positive force for kids anymore, if it ever was, and has crossed the line to harming vast numbers of children.

> **Solution:** Begin an immediate investigation of social media platforms, groups, and individuals whose intent is to influence, coach, and mold vulnerable youth, encouraging them to take drastic measures to alleviate their pain.

Problem: Excessive screen time.

> **Solution:** If your child is still a minor, consider limiting, pausing, or discontinuing social media interaction or possibly closing accounts. Prioritize in-person interaction and meaningful work and family/community involvement off-line, if possible.

Problem: Parental rights are being eroded by gender ideology, and parents are demonized for expressing concern.

It is time to cease undermining parental authority and stop encouraging young people to discard their families. Please stop devaluing the family that raised kids by saying such things as, "If your parents aren't accepting of your identity, I'm your mom now."

> **Solution:** Schools and the medical community need to remember that parents generally know their kids best. Any policy that usurps parental rights within the school or medical system needs to be flipped to acknowledge that parents

> are the key to understanding the complexity of their children's history and underlying conditions. Stop demonizing parents who desire non-medical treatment options and express concern for the lifelong consequences of harm to the health of their beloved child.
>
> Define reparations to make amends for the wrongs some have done, such as removing children from their homes because the parents used the name they lovingly chose for their son or daughter and the corresponding pronouns of their natal sex. Defining the use of a child's birth name as abusive and a cause for a child's placement in foster care is egregious.

Problem: Lack of acceptance for the natural body.

We have lost our way when we do not encourage the acceptance of the natural body in all its shapes and sizes. We have also forgotten that puberty is difficult, and we must help young people navigate it naturally.

> **Solution:** Help guide young people through puberty. Provide educational information on the changes and challenges that occur during this phase of life. Instead of encouraging youth to think they were born in the wrong body, remind them that each cell and organ in their body was coded with either XX or XY chromosomes prior to their birth, and chemicals cannot change that coding. Let's focus on promoting self-acceptance. I have hopes that young women will once again embrace their divine feminine essence and spirit and choose to honor matriarchy, the female body, and womanhood in all its beauty.

Problem: Families are torn apart by the rapid medicalization procedures.

I advocate for families ripped apart by this devastating, ideological culture. It is time to focus on the family and the rebuilding of relationships that were damaged or discarded in the throes of medicalization procedures. Trauma abounds.

> **Solution:** Let's pivot and put energy into the care and healing of the deep wounds gender ideology has created.

Problem: Therapy and mental health care are underutilized, if utilized at all.

Thank you to the brave psychiatrists, doctors, educators, counselors, and many others who are risking their careers to speak up against trans medicalization. Therapists who treat the whole person instead of focusing on one dimension—gender identity issues—are often at risk of losing their jobs or licenses. I support mental health care that takes the time to treat the true root causes of distress. Years of therapy and different types of therapy might be necessary to unravel and treat trauma and comorbidities.

> **Solution:** We need therapists to view the entire young person who sits before them. Therapy must dig deeper than the initial presentation of one's current wishes to transform their body to look like the opposite sex, which is often a sudden and transient desire and may be the result of social contagion. Underlying issues follow people around for the rest of their lives and interface with every relationship and encounter. Focus on healthy relationships, including the repair of family ties. It is unacceptable for anyone to coerce

parents and engage in emotional blackmail, such as saying their kid will commit suicide if the parent does not agree to the cross-sex medicalization of their child. It is also time to stop threatening therapists and pigeonholing them into affirmation-only therapy.

Problem: Loss of women's rights and the denigration of women and the word "woman."

Solution: Acknowledge girls and women as a sex class with sex-based rights. Return the words *woman/women* in all places where they were removed, such as literature, maternity spaces, medical references, toilets, changing/locker rooms, spas, shelters, prisons, sports, and other places. Provide safe spaces for women.

Problem: Lack of fair competition in women's sports.

Solution: Do not allow men to compete in women's sports. Make reparations for the wrongs that have occurred in the past when men have competed in women's divisions and competitions. Remove awards and titles given to trans women (biological males) and reassign to the female athletes who actually won.

Problem: The ever-increasing alphabet of LGBTQ+ and the display of rainbow flags.

Solution: Consider dropping the labeling and never-ending identification list that comes after LGB, and consider removing rainbow flags from wherever they are displayed.

It is increasingly dangerous to display controversial flags. Furthermore, both letters and flags may have originally been used to represent "inclusion," but currently, they encourage divisiveness in this controversial arena. Let all people just live and work, and children go to school, without having to publicly declare their personal sex attraction or identification. Those are private matters that do not belong in the workplace or the classroom.

Problem: Political demonization makes this a polarizing issue rather than one that needs all sides to work together.

US liberals are likely to say I have been influenced by right-wing rhetoric; however, my information is from an independent position seeped in research, science, and biology. Blame and finger-pointing abound. My solid personal belief in a higher power is not enough for most Christians. I have been told that my family mess is a result of me not raising my kids in church. I have been told more than once that I am a bad mother because I couldn't stop my daughter from harming herself. I have been blamed for not affirming my daughter's medicalization to present as a man. Some liberals proclaim that conservatives aim to harm the LGBTQ community, which negates all the Democrats and the LGB community working hard to help keep our younger generation from extreme medicalization procedures.

Solution: Political demonization needs to cease, and both parties need to work together to pass legislation and enact policy changes to protect children and young adults from drug dependency and radical surgeries.

One truth is for sure: there is controversy about and within the LGBTQ+ umbrella and the gender affirmation care model's ideals of encouraging and supporting children and young adults to attempt to change their biological, natal sex with drugs and surgery. If we look at the history of harmful ideologies and the people who follow them, those who participate in erasure may not have longevity. The gender identity ideology movement appears to wish to erase birth sex and birth names, women's rights and spaces, moms and family members who don't agree, and LGB people. The movement also seems to wish to change language and rewrite history for its purposes and not for the greater good of society and families within it that disagree with extremists' agendas. Be sure you are aware of what you affirm and how your affirmation-only stance affects others.

After extensive research on the many issues of medicalization of trans-identifying youth, I do not find it to be an acceptable treatment pathway for young people. In summary, I find these problems with gender identity ideology:

- Lack of scientific evidence for its efficacy
- Failure to address underlying trauma, relationship loss, body dysphoria, mental issues, and commonalities
- Dismissal of innate biology and lack of acceptance of the natural body
- Enabling of distorted body images, confusion, and maladaptive behaviors
- Dissolution of parental authority and dismissal of wisdom
- Encouragement to break ties with family
- Social media spaces and individuals who glamorize and encourage medicalization for young people
- Social contagion

- Cult-like behavior
- Conversion or erasure of homosexual individuals
- Sterilization of youth before they have had the chance to progress through puberty, adulthood, and child-bearing years
- Dishonoring women and the loss of women's rights and safe spaces

Let's pivot out of this harmful ideology and support our children. They have a right to move through puberty naturally without puberty blockers. They need time to mature without the adverse effects of cross-sex hormones and irreversible surgeries. They deserve an exploration of natural treatment options and healing for the distress that prompted their request to permanently alter their bodies.

Who will clean up this mess? Will insurance companies cover the repair of complications or reconstructive surgery for elective procedures to remove healthy body parts? I suspect there will be many days and years of reckoning as lawyers advocate for victims and sue people who participated in this aggressive and reckless medicalization model. Will the lawsuits be aimed at gender affirming clinics and practitioners who set these young and vulnerable kids on the trans train without asking enough (or any) questions or treating underlying conditions and comorbidities? Will the surgeons who removed healthy breasts, female reproductive organs, penises, and testicles without asking enough (or any) questions or differentiating a sex change request for inappropriate reasons (such as engaging in a fad or making a counter-cultural/stereotype statement) be sued for negligence and malpractice? Who is responsible for complications and regrets from irreversible surgery? How will we address the person who wants to have children but cannot as a result of being rendered sterile?

How will schools respond to lawsuits due to participating in children's social transition at school while hiding information from the children's parents? Will schools face repercussions for calling social service agencies and reporting parents as unsafe or abusive for calling their child by their given name and corresponding pronouns?

The future seems uncertain, but I give kudos to those brave parents and others who dare stand up in advocating for the protection of our young daughters and sons with books such as *Parents with Inconvenient Truths about Trans: Tales from the Home Front in the Fight to Save Our Kids.* Those who have never been a parent and people who have never stepped inside our homes or watched and participated in every year of our kids' lives are not qualified to judge or condemn us. It is not heroic to undermine parents.

History books are likely to look back at this dark time in our society's policies and attitudes with shock that it was allowed to continue as long as it did. I hope everyone wakes up to the reality of the great harm to our young people. The gender industry is fast becoming a medical scandal. An ideology that denies biological reality and promotes sex change surgeries that remove healthy breasts, genitalia and reproductive organs of healthy kids and young adults has gone on too long. Please, take off your blinders and help fix this blunder in human history.

The US nation's youth should not be treated as experimental subjects. Pay attention to European questioning of ethical management of young girls and women with dysphoria and the U-turn that many clinics are now making. Listen to the whistleblowers.

Please dismantle the medicalized trans train pathway. If you are a part of the affirmation-only model, please step off it and funnel your love and good intentions in a different direction. It may be difficult to shift your paradigm from your previous well-intentioned stance that may not have been serving in the capacity that you first believed you were serving. The realization that your place of employment or community might have been captured might be a big pill to swallow. It isn't easy to take ownership of being misguided and adjust what you had been saying and doing. Evaluate the gender medicalization industry and philosophies carefully. Thank you to anyone who considers that parental insight and wisdom might be important to consider when making policies or a diagnosis and treatment plan.

It was difficult to write a book that revealed personal and family matters. I would prefer to live in relative obscurity, but I felt compelled to speak up. Publicly exposing my deepest pain is not my idea of a good time. I do not believe we were meant to mess with nature and God's delicate design of the male and female bodies. I trust that a rational, heart-centered, passionate perspective comes through in my words. I am a parent leading with love and wisdom that come from age and experience.

I have much healing to do in recovering from the most devastating and traumatic event of my life: losing my daughter to the trans train. I will need to practice forgiveness of those who distanced themselves from me when I most needed their support and for those who championed the rapid medicalization of my daughter. It will take time to desensitize myself from the sting of being called a transphobe and the feeling of being minimized or undermined when I said the trans medicalization pipeline wasn't good for our kids.

I hold hope that my words will be supportive to the community of brokenhearted parents out there, and perhaps those devastated readers will feel less alone in their agony of loss. I hope to hear from anyone who feels the book resonated with them. I stand with those in the LGB community who have been kind and who have also been targets of hateful rhetoric and threats by trans activists. I realize that not all trans-identifying people are in favor of the medicalization of minors and young adults, as the organization LGBT Courage Coalition seems to indicate. On their Substack, they say, "Lesbian, gay, bisexual, and transgender adults concerned with pediatric gender medicine and the censorship of dissent. We won't be silenced." Thank you to any transsexual person who bravely raises awareness of their concerns regarding the medicalization processes.

Perhaps my readers now have more knowledge about what is happening within the trans train movement. I hope you will connect with the resources at the back of this book and become involved in some way for positive change. Others have started to pave the road ahead, and if we work together, we can make changes. There are things you can do. Please join me and become involved in the worthy organizations that are already set up to support you. We can make a difference. No matter your party affiliation, consider participating in reform and vote for legislation that protects the bodies of our younger generation. I appreciate those who share this book and message with others as a way to understand a parent's perspective.

The views in this book are my own, but I also attempted to give voice to other parents, groups, and individuals. We may not have complete alignment in our beliefs, but my intention is to bring the reader greater awareness of the controversy surrounding gender ideology.

I choose to speak up instead of acquiescing to the demands to be quiet. May your new knowledge and expanding awareness empower you to stand strong within your own life and circumstances. Exercise your voice. Share your wisdom.

Well-meaning people often rally for social justice issues, particularly new ones. However, if you are on the sidelines of trans medicalization, be cautious before giving blanket support without looking inside it. Parents lose count of the number of dismissive remarks they have received regarding losing a child in this manner. Most dismissive comments come from those who have not done any research on what is really going on in this medicalization trend. Perhaps this book has brought to light more concepts to consider as you interact with those who have a loved one caught up in it.

If you are reading this book and you are not a parent or have not lost a child to "trans" medicalization, I have suggestions for you.

- Avoid giving a grieving parent advice. Your intentions might come from a caring place, but they make us feel worse because those suggestions might show us just how much you do not understand us and what is happening. Unless we ask you directly for guidance, do not say, "You should …"
- The question, "Are you in therapy?" might come from a loving place but feels off to us if it implies that we are the problem or that you don't want to hear about it. Perhaps ask how we are caring for ourselves during this difficult time instead.
- Avoid trying to normalize or minimize our situation or our loss. Nothing in our world is normal when a generation of kids, their schoolteachers, counselors, the medical system, and media all ignore our kids' underlying pain or mental issues and instead encourage and affirm kids with their delusion that they can change their natal sex to fix their problems.
- Do not ask us to participate in or push medicalization, thereby making our kids drug-dependent, surgically altered, and unrecognizable to us. Do not ask us to affirm our children's self-identification of trans that likely came from a destructive social contagion or zealous social media influencers when

they were most vulnerable. Do not ask us to celebrate our kids cutting off healthy body parts.

- Please stop politicalizing or participating with any ideology that vocalizes that parents are abusive, hateful transphobes because we express concerns, ask questions, and prefer other options or therapy over drugs and surgery that forever alter our children's bodies.
- Avoid starting a conversation with "How are you?" Instead, say something like, "It is good to see you" or "It's good to hear your voice" if by phone. You might also say, "I have been thinking of you." Then, just be quiet and let us respond and direct the dialogue in a way we can handle. "How are you?" is conventional in greetings, but it forces us to cringe or lie, and it just doesn't work for us as we mourn.
- Join us for a cup of coffee, a meal, a walk, a movie, or something you know we like to do. We are traumatized and grieving. We are very alone and in despair. Practice witnessing the depth of our pain without running in the opposite direction of our needs. Someday, you might just find yourself in a similar place due to any number of circumstances. Your ability to be with us in our darkest hour is a gift to us.

What You Can Do to Help

1. Read the resources, and if one resonates with you, dig in and also share it.
2. If this book offered value, spread the word. Purchase additional copies to give to others. Consider writing a book review.

3. If you are on a social media platform, share this book or other resources with your following and within groups.
4. Ask questions when you have them and dare to bring up concerns when you see them.
5. Be cautious of supporting and enabling quick fixes such as cross-sex hormone dependency and surgical interventions for our children, teens, and young adults.
6. Advocate digging deeper and treating the confusion, emotional pain, trauma, abuse, or illness of our vulnerable young people.
7. Refresh yourself in science, biology, and sound research.
8. Utilize your strengths to add to the advocacy of helping young girls, boys, women, and men who struggle with sexual identity find better care than the gender affirmation care model. Look into Genspect as a starting point.
9. Participate in policy changes and social media reform that make medicalization the last option of treatment after years of other measures to care for the whole person and not just one facet of gender.
10. Support and be kind to traumatized and grieving parents or family members who have lost a child to this tragedy.

History shows that mothers can be a force for good and for change. Borrowing from the mission of Mothers Against Drunk Driving,[57] please volunteer, take action, support, and fundraise. We must stop the harm befalling our children from puberty blockers, cross-sex hormones, and irreversible surgeries that damage their bodies, their health, and their future well-being.

"It doesn't matter how strong your opinions are.
If you don't use your power for positive change, you are,
indeed, part of the problem."
— Coretta Scott King

My daughter has chosen a pathway of extreme divergence from her womanhood and all that it represents. I stand firm in my love and allow her autonomy to do what she wants with her body and her life. She will have to take ownership of her future and responsibility for her choices.

From my perspective, as her mom, transgender ideology swallowed her up, and the end result was a person that I, Mom, no longer know or recognize. I, too, have the autonomy to speak up and express my thoughts, my values, and my opinions about an ideology that seems to be harming a multitude of individuals and groups.

My life is full of people and things I love to do, and I will carry on as my own person, which has turned out quite differently from the life I once envisioned when I first became a mother. This book concludes, but the story isn't over. Signing off in hopes of a better future and a better ending to this story in the years to come.

— Lisa Shultz

"You may not control all the events that happen to you, but
you can decide not to be reduced by them."
— Maya Angelou

Acknowledgments

THIS BOOK WAS PAINFUL TO WRITE. I was alone in my research and writing of it. Putting thoughts and feelings down on paper in an organized manner about this controversial topic was not easy; however, the project helped me crawl out of the darkest point of my life and find meaning by bringing awareness of the complexity of gender ideology and by supporting other devastated parents.

> *"The final stage of healing is using what happens to you to help other people. That is healing in itself."*
>
> — Gloria Steinem

I had to be careful about who I told about the book during the writing process. During conversations, I sometimes ran into someone in the affirmation camp, and I realized I would need to limit my conversation with those who wanted me to surrender and accept the loss and my daughter's trans identity without question.

I was inspired by other brave parents and others who dared to vocalize their distress about the trans train. When I read Jennifer Wesson's piece, *The Gender Party*, I began sharing it with a few select friends. Several people said that it echoed all I had been telling them. I immediately knew that I wanted the entire article included in my book and asked for and received permission to feature it in my book. Thank you, Jennifer, for your valuable contribution.

I deeply thank my inner circle, who witnessed my pain and supported me. I apologize to those I did not tell and those I stepped away from during the process of writing this book.

I thank my parents, whose solid values live on beyond their deaths and guided me as I wrote.

I thank my devoted and dedicated publishing team. You are the best!

To my trans-identified daughter, I hope one day that you will come to see that this book was my attempt to say that I love you so much that I was willing to challenge an ideological movement that captured you. I love you from the depths of my being and my heart. Even if your outward appearance is unrecognizable, I see your beautiful inner essence and spirit.

About the Author

LISA SHULTZ earned a science-based university degree and enjoyed a career in medical care before she retired to become a full-time, stay-at-home mom. After her kids went off to universities and beyond, she shifted her focus to that of a writer. She is dedicated to upholding women's rights and preserving their natural bodies, spaces, and dignity.

Find additional resources at LisaShultz.com. If you wish to share a story with the author, email: TheTransTrain2024@gmail.com.

Resources

The list of resources changes and grows frequently. For an updated list, including parent support groups, visit LisaShultz.com.

ORGANIZATIONS

4th Wave Now

A community of people who question the medicalization of gender-atypical youth.

https://4thwavenow.com

Beyond Trans

Beyond Trans offers funding for therapy and provides free therapeutic programs to people who feel distressed or ambivalent about their transition.

https://beyondtrans.org

Biological Integrity

Biological Integrity is a reliable medical resource on the topic of gender dysphoria for parents, teens, physicians, schools, and policymakers. It is a Project of the American College of Pediatricians.

https://biologicalintegrity.org

Do No Harm

A diverse group of physicians, healthcare professionals, medical students, patients, and policymakers united by a moral mission: Protect healthcare from a radical, divisive, and discriminatory ideology. They believe in making healthcare better for all—not undermining it in pursuit of a political agenda.

https://donoharmmedicine.org

Gender Dysphoria Support Network

The Gender Dysphoria Support Network (GDSN) is an international group that aims to offer support to families of individuals affected by gender dysphoria. International parent support group information and other resources are available.

https://genderdysphoriasupportnetwork.com

Genspect

Genspect is an international organization that promotes a healthy approach to sex and gender. Their team includes professionals, trans-identifying people, detransitioners, and parent groups who campaign for high-quality care for gender-related distress. They advocate for a non-medicalized approach to gender diversity.

https://genspect.org

Parents around the world are speaking:
https://genspect.org/resources/parent-stories/

LGBT Courage Coalition

Lesbian, gay, bisexual, and transgender adults concerned with pediatric gender medicine and the censorship of dissent.

https://lgbtcouragecoalition.substack.com/

Our Duty

Our Duty is an international support network for parents who wish to protect their children from gender ideology.

https://ourduty.group

Paradox Institute

The Paradox Institute believes that the denial of the two sexes is one of the fundamental issues of our time. It has never been more important to have an educated public on how sex differences impact individuals and society. Understanding the sexes is critical for psychological health, social relationships, accurate medical research, correct reporting of crime statistics, fairness and safety in sports, and ultimately, the health of our societies and the continuation of our species. Learn more about how affirmation care harms children and teens and much more.

https://www.theparadoxinstitute.com

Parents with Inconvenient Truths about Trans (PITT)

PITT is a space for parents who have been impacted by gender ideology to share their uncensored stories, experiences, and thoughts while remaining anonymous to protect themselves and their families.

Their objective is to inform the public about the devastating impact of gender ideology on families through their personal experiences.

https://pitt.substack.com

Partners for Ethical Care

Partners for Ethical Care is a secular, non-partisan, all-volunteer, grassroots nonprofit organization comprised of individuals from across the globe. Their mission is to raise awareness and support efforts to stop the unethical treatment of children by schools, hospitals, and mental and medical healthcare providers under the duplicitous banner of gender identity affirmation.

https://www.partnersforethicalcare.com

Post Trans

Post Trans is a project that aims to give visibility and support to female detransitioners. Read a collection of detrans stories from female detransitioners and desisters.

https://post-trans.com

Rethink Identity Medicine Ethics (ReIME)

ReIME supports the rights of minors and young people to explore identities, including sexualities and genders, that are developmentally appropriate. They believe the standards of care and treatment protocols for this vulnerable population should be informed by well-researched and evidence-based best practices for addressing complex developmental and dysphoric issues related to identity and the body on an individual, case-by-case basis.

https://rethinkime.org

Sex Change Regret

Sex Change Regret provides evidence, resources, and support for those considering detransitioning. This organization's website states, "Up to 20% have regrets about their 'sex change.' Sex change procedures are not effective, say researchers. Ten to 15 years after surgical reassignment, the suicide rate is 20 times that of comparable peers. Regret is NOT rare."

http://sexchangeregret.com

Sex Matters

A human rights organization that believes sex matters in law and in life.

https://sex-matters.org

Society for Evidence-Based Gender Medicine (SEGM)

SEGM is an international group of clinicians and researchers concerned with the lack of quality evidence for the use of hormonal and surgical interventions as first-line treatment for young people with gender dysphoria. Their aim is to promote safe, compassionate, ethical, and evidence-informed healthcare for children, adolescents, and young adults with gender dysphoria.

https://segm.org

The Transition Justice Project

The Transition Justice Project helps connect detransitioners and others who have had negative effects of gender medicine to connect with legal assistance.

https://www.transitionjustice.org

Themis Resource Fund

This fund connects detransitioned plaintiffs to legal resources.

https://themisresourcefund.org

Therapy First

Therapy First is a nonprofit professional association of over three hundred mental health providers worldwide who view psychotherapy as the appropriate first-line treatment for gender dysphoria. They aim to support psychotherapists working with gender dysphoric children, adolescents, and young adults in providing high-quality, evidence-based mental health care and to offer public education on mental health and psychotherapy.

https://www.therapyfirst.org

Thoughtful Therapists

This group from the UK and Ireland has come together with a shared concern about the impact of gender identity ideology on children and young people. https://thoughtfultherapists.org

Transgender Trend

Transgender Trend, an organization based in the UK with no religious or political affiliation, is comprised of parents, professionals, and academics. They believe that there is "no reliable scientific basis for the diagnosis of transgender, nor long-term research on the outcome of treatments. Setting children off on a path toward medicalisation with irreversible lifelong effects is an experiment which has no precedent."

https://www.transgendertrend.com

Women Are Real

This website supports women. They say, "We are women—Liberal, Moderate, and Conservative—who believe that sex still matters in daily lives of women and girls."

- Women deserve dignity and safety in sports, locker rooms, prisons, and shelters.
- When anyone can self-identify into women-only spaces, these spaces are no longer single-sex.
- Trans-identified people must have civil rights, such as protection from housing and employment discrimination, but those rights need not come at a cost to women's safety and dignity.

https://womenarereal.org

Women's Declaration International (WDI)

WDI is a group of volunteer women from across the globe dedicated to protecting women's sex-based rights. The Declaration of Women's Sex-Based Rights reaffirms women and girls' sex-based rights and challenges discrimination from the replacement of the category of sex with that of "gender identity."

https://www.womensdeclaration.com

BOOKS

DETRANS: When Transition Is Not the Solution, Dr. Az Hakeem

TRANS: Exploring Gender Identity and Gender Dysphoria, Dr. Az Hakeem

Irreversible Damage: The Transgender Craze Seducing Our Daughters, Abigail Shrier

When Kids Say They're Trans: A Guide for Parents, Lisa Marchian, Stella O'Malley

Lost in Trans Nation: A Child Psychiatrist's Guide Out of the Madness, Miriam Grossman, MD

Parents with Inconvenient Truths about Trans: Tales from the Home Front in the Fight to Save Our Kids, Josie A., Dina S.

The Abolition of Sex: How the "Transgender" Agenda Harms Women and Girls, Kara Dansky

The Reckoning: How the Democrats and the Left Betrayed Women and Girls, Kara Dansky

Time to Think: The Inside Story of the Collapse of the Tavistock's Gender Service for Children, Hannah Barnes

Trans: When Ideology Meets Reality, Helen Joyce

I Am Not Sick, I Don't Need Help!, Dr. Xavier Amador
This book is not about the trans topic, but the LEAP technique presented is a powerful communication tool that can transform difficult relationships.

FILMS

The Detransition Diaries: Saving Our Sisters
https://vimeo.com/ondemand/detransitiondiaries

Gender Transformation: The Untold Realities
https://www.gendertransformation.com

No Way Back: The Reality of Gender Affirming Care
https://nowaybackfilm.com

Uncomfortable Truths: The Reality of Gender Identity Ideology
https://www.thesignalproductions.com

PODCAST

Gender: A Wider Lens
https://genspect.org/widerlens/

SHORT DOCUMENTARY

Detrans: The Dangers of Gender-Affirming Care
https://www.prageru.com/video/detrans

INTERNATIONAL GROUPS

- 4th Wave Now
- Gender Dysphoria Alliance
- Gender Health Query
- Institute for Comprehensive Gender Dysphoria Research

- LGB Alliance – has groups in Australia, Brazil, Canada, Germany, Iceland, Ireland, Mexico, Norway, Poland, Scotland, Serbia, Spain, the US and Wales.
- PITT (Parents with Inconvenient Truths about Trans)
- Post-trans
- Rethink Identity Medicine Ethics
- Society of Evidence-Based Gender Medicine
- Therapy First
- Thoughtful Therapists
- Trans Widows Voices
- Clinical Advisory Network on Sex and Gender-has groups in Ireland & the UK.

INTERNATIONAL GROUPS BY COUNTRY

- Canada – Canadian Gender Report
- France – La Petite Sirène
- Norway – Harry Benjamin Ressurssenter
- UK – dsdfamilies
- UK – Safe Schools Alliance
- UK – Sex Matters
- UK – Transgender Trend
- US – Child and Parental Rights Campaign

The list of resources changes and grows frequently. For an updated list, including parent support groups, visit LisaShultz.com.

Endnotes

1 "Legal action may change transgender care in America," The Economist, March 7, 2023, https://www.economist.com/united-states/2023/03/07/legal-action-may-change-transgender-care-in-america.

2 James Esses on Substack, https://www.jamesesses.com/.

3 Jay W. Richards, "What Is Gender Ideology?" The Heritage Foundation, July 7, 2023, https://www.heritage.org/gender/commentary/what-gender-ideology.

4 "Sweden's U-Turn on Trans Kids: The Trans Train (Part 1): The New Patient Group & Regretters," Thoughts on Things and Stuff, YouTube, January 16, 2023, https://www.youtube.com/watch?v=MVEZ7gELcgY&t=0s.

5 "Transition Roadmap," UCSF Transgender Care, University of California, San Francisco, https://transcare.ucsf.edu/transition-roadmap.

6 Paul C. Gregory, Peer Reviewed by Chris Drew, "12 Medicalization Examples," Helpful Professor, August 25, 2023, https://helpfulprofessor.com/medicalization-examples/#.

7 Robert Withers, "Transgender medicalization and the attempt to evade psychological distress," The Journal of Analytical Psychology, November 17, 2020, https://www.ncbi.nlm.nih.gov/pmc/articles/PMC7787368/.

8 "Glitter family" definition, bannedfromfacebookagain, Urban Dictionary, May 9, 2023, https://www.urbandictionary.com/define.php?term=glitter%20family.

9 "Study of 1,655 Cases Supports the 'Rapid-Onset Gender Dysphoria' Hypothesis," Society for Evidence Based Gender Medicine, last modified November 18, 2023, https://segm.org/study-of-1655-cases-lends-support-to-ROGD.

10 "How Many Genders Are There? Gender Identity List," Sexual Diversity, last modified May 22, 2023, https://www.sexualdiversity.org/edu/1111.php.

11 "LGBTQ Terms and Definitions," LGBTQ+ Services, Loyola University Maryland, https://www.loyola.edu/department/lgbtq-services/resources/lgbtq-terms-definitions.

12 LGB Alliance, https://lgballiance.org.uk.

13 LGB Alliance, https://lgbausa.org.

14 "Trans ideology has caused a 'lot of tragedy' for lesbians," Sky News Australia, YouTube, June 1, 2023, https://www.youtube.com/watch?v=cD5px59nXy8.

15 Ben Appel, "The New Homophobia," Newsweek, April 21, 2022, https://www.newsweek.com/new-homophobia-opinion-1698969.

16 Ben Appel, "Homophobia in drag," Spiked, May 14, 2023, https://www.spiked-online.com/2023/05/14/the-new-homophobia/.

17 "Transsexualism vs. Transgenderism: A Personal Reflection," Tired Transsexual, September 25, 2023, https://www.tiredtrans-sexual.com/p/transsexualism-vs-transgenderism.

18 Mariam Arain, Maliha Hague, Lina Johal, Poja Mathur, Wynand Nel, Afsha Rais, Ranbir Sandhu, and Sushil Sharma, "Maturation of the adolescent brain," Neuropsychiatric Disease and Treatment 2013; 9: 449-461, April 3, 2013, National Library of Medicine, https://www.ncbi.nlm.nih.gov/pmc/articles/PMC3621648/.

19 "Exposed: The Darkside of De-transitioning," PBD Podcast, YouTube, November 11, 2023, https://www.youtube.com/watch?v=FJFj0ojmk8Q&t=3260s.

20 "Trans Ideology is the New Homophobia: Arielle Scarcella," Triggernometry, YouTube, June 15, 2022, https://www.youtube.com/watch?v=NrH-W9XfOj8.

21 Miriam Grossman, *Lost in Trans Nation: A Child Psychiatrist's Guide Out of the Madness* (Skyhorse Publishing, 2023), https://a.co/d/imcEu9d.

22 James Esses, "Where Do You Fall On The Wheel of Privilege?" James Esses on Substack, August 30, 2023, https://www.jamesesses.com/p/where-do-you-fall-on-the-wheel-of.

23 "'I wish I could feel my chest': Ex-trans shares her story," Andy Ngo Live, YouTube, November 1, 2022, https://www.youtube.com/watch?v=p90K88EdOXs.

24 "Queer," Wikipedia, last modified January 10, 2024, https://en.wikipedia.org/wiki/Queer.

25 "Queer Theory: A Rough Introduction," Illinois Library, last updated November 9, 2023, https://guides.library.illinois.edu/queertheory/background.

26 WebMD Editorial Contributors, medically reviewed by Gabriela Pichardo, "What Is Fluid?" WebMD, July 2, 2023, https://www.webmd.com/sex/what-is-fluid.

27 "Trigender," Wikipedia, last modified January 13, 2024, https://simple.wikipedia.org/wiki/Trigender.

28 Post Trans, https://post-trans.com.

29 Detransition 17, Post Trans, https://post-trans.com/Detransition-17.

30 Detransition 6, Post Trans, https://post-trans.com/Detransition-6.

31 Eli, Detransition 5, "Transition was a means of escape," Post Trans, https://post-trans.com/Detransition-Eli-5.

32 Ellie, Detransition 1, "What detransition means to me," Post Trans, https://post-trans.com/Detransition-Ellie-1.

33 r/detrains thread, Reddit, https://www.reddit.com/r/detrans/.

34 Wokal Distance, "Ideological Capture," Keep your Wokal distance, October 21, 2022, https://wokaldistance.substack.com/p/ideological-capture.

35 Susan Jane Bradley, "Understanding Vulnerability in Girls and Young Women with High-Functioning Autism Spectrum Disorder," *Women* 2, no. 1: 64-67, https://www.mdpi.com/2673-4184/2/1/7.

36 "An interview with Dr. Az Hakeem," Transgender Trend, September 1, 2021, https://www.transgendertrend.com/interview-az-hakeem/.

37 "How Much Does Top Surgery Cost?" Top Surgery, last updated September 21, 2023, https://www.topsurgery.net/costs/.

38 "U.S. Sex Reassignment Surgery Market to Reach $5.0 Billion by 2030," Grand View Research, August 2023, https://www.grandviewresearch.com/press-release/us-sex-reassignment-surgery-market-analysis.

39 Sumant Ugalmugl and Rupali Swain, "Sex Reassignment Surgery Market size to exceed $1.95Bn by 2032," Global Market Insights, February 9, 2023, https://www.gminsights.com/pressrelease/sex-reassignment-surgery-market.

40 “Archived – Affirming services,” Ontario, last updated February 11, 2022, https://www.ontario.ca/document/serving-lgbt2sq-children-and-youth-child-welfare-system/affirming-services.

41 Michael Knowles, “A Story of Detransitioning,” Michael Knowles, YouTube, March 25, 2022, https://www.youtube.com/watch?v=5HbPzJy9gkY.

42 Peak Trans!, https://www.peaktrans.org.

43 Jamie Reed, “I Thought I Was Saving Trans Kids. Now I’m Blowing the Whistle,” The Free Press, February 9, 2023, https://www.thefp.com/p/i-thought-i-was-saving-trans-kids.

44 “Trans Clinic Whistleblower Speaks Out,” Triggernometry, YouTube, April 16, 2023, https://www.youtube.com/watch?v=gbuGMbqjsSw.

45 “Affidavit of Jamie Reed,” February 7, 2023, https://ago.mo.gov/wp-content/uploads/2-07-2023-reed-affidavit-signed.pdf.

46 “Mom Explains What It Took to Rescue Daughter from Transgenderism,” The Daily Signal, YouTube, January 30, 2023, https://www.youtube.com/watch?v=z1oh4dsbsb4.

47 https://www.wbur.org/onpoint/2023/03/09/the-inside-story-of-the-collapse-of-the-tavistock-gender-service-for-children#.

48 Marcus Evans, “Why I Resigned from Tavistock: Trans-Identified Children Need Therapy, Not Just ‘Affirmation’ and Dr,” Quillette, January 17, 2020, https://www.researchgate.net/publication/338885615_Why_I_Resigned_from_

Tavistock_Trans-Identified_Children_Need_Therapy_Not_Just_%27Affirmation%27_and_Dr.

49 James Esses, https://www.jamesesses.com/.

50 Leor Sapir, Manhattan Institute, https://manhattan.institute/person/leor-sapir.

51 "Sex Is Binary," Colin Wright, PragerU, YouTube, September 18, 2023, https://drcolinwright.com; https://www.youtube.com/watch?v=1dAo0RJTiKU.

52 The Riley Gaines Center at the Leadership Institute, https://rileygainescenter.org.

53 "Biologically Male Transsexual TEARS Into Radicals Attacking Women's Sports," The Daily Signal, YouTube, January 24, 2022, https://www.youtube.com/watch?v=G8lgScZ0YzY.

54 Emily Chudy, "JK Rowling says she knew trans views would make Harry Potter fans 'unhappy': 'It has not been fun,' PinkNews, March 15, 2023, https://www.thepinknews.com/2023/03/15/jk-rowling-podcast-trans-views-fan-backlash/.

55 r/detrains thread, Reddit, https://www.reddit.com/r/detrans/.

56 Society for Evidence Based Gender Medicine, https://segm.org.

57 Mothers Against Drunk Driving (MADD), https://madd.org.

Made in the USA
Coppell, TX
25 February 2024